RIO
FERDINAND

World Cup Heroes.

RIO FERDINAND

Wensley Clarkson

JB

JOHN BLAKE

Published by John Blake Publishing Ltd,
3 Bramber Court, 2 Bramber Road,
London W14 9PB, England

www.johnblakepublishing.co.uk

This edition published in 2010

ISBN: 978 1 84358 177 2

British Library Cataloguing-in-Publication Data:

A catalogue record for this book is available from the British Library.

Design by www.envydesign.co.uk

Printed in Great Britain by CPI Bookmarque, Croydon CR0 4TD

1 3 5 7 9 10 8 6 4 2

Papers used by John Blake Publishing are natural, recyclable products
made from wood grown in sustainable forests. The manufacturing processes
conform to the environmental regulations of the country of origin.

1

Pregnant teenager Janice Lavender knew within days of arriving on the Friary Estate in Peckham, south-east London, that any son of hers would need constant supervision if he was going to stay out of trouble. Muggings, burglaries and violence were a feature of daily life. People rarely ventured out at night because they were terrified they might encounter one of the many gangs of youths who patrolled the area. At the only shop on the estate the owner had metal shutters over the windows, but they were regularly prised open. All boys needed watching, cajoling and hauling into line. Only responsible, caring parents stood a chance of seeing their kids survive this environment.

Janice moved into a block called Gisburn House, a grim four-storey, red-brick council tenement building which overlooked rusting cars and a couple of burned-out white Transit vans. The flat that would become Rio Ferdinand's home for the first 18 years of his life was up four flights of narrow, dirty, urine-smelling stairs. Its red-framed front door was secured behind black metal bars. The flat was small, with threadbare carpet, sparse furniture and walls badly in need of a new coat of paint. The cramped second bedroom contained just a bed. Lack of wardrobe space meant that clothes had to be hung from door frames. But for Rio it would become a place of comfort and safety, an escape from the fear that came with running the gauntlet through the estate.

These conditions didn't faze Janice. She was one of 11 children whose Irish mother left home when she was young, and she was determined her own kids wouldn't suffer the same fate. 'My dad did a wonderful job in bringing us up but I can never remember being spoiled,' she recalled. She had left home at 15 and took a job at Top Shop in Oxford Street, in London's West End, to help pay the rent on her bedsit. When she was just 17 she got pregnant after starting a relationship with St Lucia-born Julian Ferdinand, whose family had arrived in Britain from the Caribbean in 1958.

Janice's baby boy was born at King's College Hospital, Camberwell, south London, on 7 November 1978. He was almost named Gavin but his mother Janice and father Julian both preferred Rio, after the Rio Grande, so Gavin became his middle name. The young parents never married, and for Janice: 'It was a big shock to come home with Rio. That tiny two-bedroom flat on the fourth floor was freezing. And back in those days it was quite a thing that Rio's dad was black and I was white.'

The National Front were still active and there was a lot of animosity shown to Janice and her tiny, milky-coffee-coloured baby. 'There was one particular person who would call us names – but as a woman with a baby, what do you do? There was me, this white woman, with a black child. I was so proud of him and I wanted him to look perfect every minute.'

The teenage mum was shown the ropes of estate life by single parents Sharon McEwan from Grenada and Dallas Gopie from Guyana. Janice remembered: 'At the end of a week when we didn't have much food or money left we'd pool together and feed the kids with something – rice, chicken, anything that was cheap.'

As soon as she could return to her job at Top Shop, Janice got little Rio into a nearby nursery school. She was determined to be a good role model to her son. 'I wanted my kids to know there's a big world out there with lots of things to do – but you have to work hard to get there. It was about Rio seeing that you have to work hard to make a better life for yourself.'

Janice eventually became a childminder so that she could keep earning a living but spend more time with Rio. Any spare cash soon went on sending her sports-mad son on after-school activities and even occasional holidays. There was a sports shop in Peckham called Mark One, where Janice would take the boy. 'The lady knew my situation and used to take us through to the cheap section we could afford. I always said to Rio, "It's not what you've got, it's what you do with it."'

When Rio was about six years old, Janice took him to see Liverpool take on Millwall at the Den, just a few minutes away from the Friary Estate. 'It was the most wicked thing in my life,' Rio remembered. 'The crowd was noisy. The players seemed like gods out there. I was drawn right into it.' Rio elevated Liverpool's John Barnes to the status of superhero as his goal helped the Reds scrape through 2–1.

That trip to the Den sparked Rio's obsession with football and he was soon kicking a ball around on the two concrete playgrounds at his junior school, Camelot Primary, in Peckham. Rio's former headmistress, Joye Manyan, recalled: 'He was a tall lad and would play football whenever he was allowed to. He scored goals back then, too.' In class, Rio proved to have a lively sense of humour and a good grasp of maths. 'I remember seeing him take care of a complicated question about fractions when he was just six. His mental arithmetic was good,' Mrs Manyan added.

Most afternoons after school, Rio went for a kick-about with kids and their mums in the nearby park, just yards from a procession of drug dealers plying their goods to local youths. No one hung around in the evening because the area was renowned for street robberies. Sometimes, if it was still light, the youngster would turn a piece of balding grass in front of Gisburn House into his own Wembley Stadium. 'I'd charge around the place with an imaginary voice saying in my ear, "And it's another great pass from Ferdinand under the Twin Towers ..."'

Rio formed a close attachment to his grandmother Angelina Ferdinand, who lived in a two-bedroomed terraced house just a few minutes' walk from the Friary Estate. She recalled: 'I made Rio Caribbean delicacies and told him stories about my childhood in St Lucia. Rio had a real sweet tooth and I loved making him biscuits as well.' Rio often kicked a football about on the green outside Angelina's home with her husband Raymond but football wasn't so popular with Rio's dad, Julian, who, although he never married Janice, remained very close to his son and was a strong influence throughout his early childhood. Julian encouraged Rio to take up gymnastics at school and Rio was awarded a British Amateur Gymnastics Association Class Two certificate just before his ninth birthday.

He also took ballet classes at school, but when he was nine and a half he and his dad were called in and told he would have to cut down on the dancing and gymnastics because he was growing so quickly some of his ligaments couldn't cope with the sort of movements required. That meant playing even more football.

The driving force behind Rio's search for a better life went beyond adoring football. Now, looking back on those childhood days, he admits: 'I always wanted to be a footballer but, to be honest about it, I wanted to make big money and, most of all, I wanted to be famous. I wanted to be a singer – still do – an actor, a dancer and a gymnast. I wanted to be famous.'

After being advised to quit gymnastics Rio became more focused on his football. 'I became quite scared that I wouldn't make it,' he said. 'It was a pride thing. Even now, when everyone is telling me I've made it, I can't think of it like that.' For the following couple of years, he played in the Blackheath and District Schools League and when he was 11 his skills were recognised by his uncle, Dave Raynor, who ran a Sunday-morning under-12s team called Bloomfield Athletic, in Peckham. 'He was a natural,' Raynor said. 'I didn't even have to teach him football, I just guided him. He knew how to read the game.'

Rio also caught the attention of Dave Goodwin, who

ran the Blackheath and District Schools League. Goodwin's reaction to the youngster's talents was instantaneous: 'I first saw Rio at 11 in a trial and already he looked like a seasoned pro. There were three main things that stuck out – his ability to pass the ball, the sheer vision he displayed and the way he organised a midfield.' Other people were also taking notice, including scouts from some of the big London clubs.

2

Just before his 12th birthday, Rio started attending Bluecoat Comprehensive School in Blackheath. Located just off a pokey backstreet and hidden behind a Shell petrol station, it was just two minutes up the road from unfashionable Charlton Athletic. Rio learned many of his basic soccer skills on the field next to the sadly neglected school sports hut. Angela Rezki, Rio's sports tutor throughout much of his time at Bluecoat, remembers clearly: 'Rio was so talented we all knew he would make it at football even though he was a bit of a Jack the Lad and fancied himself a bit.' She noticed that he knocked around with a group of rowdy older boys and for a while many people at the school feared that he could end up dealing drugs on the streets. 'He got into a bit of trouble, like all kids do, but his mum kept him on the straight and narrow.'

Soon Rio's football performances at weekends were the talk of the area. Here was a tall, awkward midfielder capable of some fine trickery on the ball. As well as his uncle's team and Goodwin's district side, Rio also played for a Sunday-morning outfit called Eltham Town, whose coach Paul Caldwell explained: 'The thing about Rio which was very unusual was that, apart from being the best player by far, he also had the best attitude. Normally, if you get the really skilful players, they can let it go to their heads but Rio was never like that.'

Before long Rio noticed that although the teams he played for were made up mainly of black kids, they nearly always found themselves playing predominantly white sides. A lot of the dads would come down from the pubs after lunch to cheer on their kids, but the problem was that many of them started talking about 'black this' and 'black that'. Rio had heard all sorts of insults on the streets of Peckham, but it seemed even more out of order to hear them on a football pitch. He tried to blank out all the insults and say to himself, 'Yes, I'm black and proud of it.' But there were certainly times when he was tempted to lash out at the bigots.

Every evening around 6.30 Janice would walk out of her front door, lean over the balcony and start hollering across the estate: 'REE-OOH! REE-OOH!' A brief period of silence would follow then Rio would tell his mates he had to go. 'Come on, Rio,' one of them would often plead. Rio would then hesitate.

'REE-OOH! REE-OOH!'

By the time he'd heard Janice's voice for the fourth time, the lad knew he had no choice and would scarper off in her direction. But one evening he got a bit rebellious and didn't answer his mum's rallying call. 'Then my dad came for me. We could see him walking through the estate, my mates were going, "Oh no, Rio, there's your dad. Oh my God, your dad." When he saw me, Dad just turned back towards

home. He knew I would follow. You can imagine what happened when I got home.'

It was a strict home. The arguments between disciplinarian Janice and Rio sometimes reduced the youngster to tears. But he admitted: 'Those rules were for my own good. My parents never said to me, "Don't smoke. Don't take drugs." They just left that to me. Still, if I had tried it, I'd have had to answer to my dad. But there was never anything in it for me. I was always so into sport I couldn't understand why you'd do something that wasn't good for your body.'

One night not long after his 12th birthday Rio and his six-year-old brother Anton were tucked up in their bunk beds when their parents started one of their regular shouting matches. Rio lay there trembling as the yelling got louder and louder. His dad sounded completely out of control and he heard his mum dashing out of the lounge. The old man was on her tail, towering over her. The ranting and raving started again then Julian turned around and walked towards the bedroom. The flat went deathly quiet. A few moments later he emerged from the bedroom with a sports bag in his hand. 'I gotta go, I've had enough,' he told Janice. Rio cried himself to sleep that night but made sure no one saw his tears. That was Rio's way of dealing with things – however painful they might be.

Janice was determined to keep her kids on the rails. Young Rio was about to hit his teens and it was essential he avoided trouble if he was to work his way out of the ghetto. Growing up on one of the toughest council estates in Europe was never going to be easy. At school he was picked on a lot because of his mixed-race background. A few black kids hated him as much as the white ones because he simply didn't fit in. But Rio ignored the tension and made an effort to get along with everyone, whatever their colour, race, creed or opinions, which helped him thrive in that tough environment.

One night Janice was fearful for Rio's safety after her customary shouts of 'Ree-ooh! Ree-ooh!' got no response around the estate. There had been a spate of vicious muggings by gangs of older youths in recent weeks and the parents of all younger kids were being extra vigilant. So Janice began roaming the shadowy, badly lit estate trying to find her son. Eventually she bumped into one of his friends who told her that he was 'at Ahmed's house'. Janice takes up the story: 'Sure enough there he was, watching a really important game of Italian football. I couldn't believe it – he hadn't asked me if he could go out. Well, he couldn't get off the chair; you could see he was scared because he knew I'd smack him.' Not even Rio the charmer, who'd been so outgoing since a young age, could talk his way out of this little spot of bother.

Matt Delaney, Rio's PE teacher at Bluecoat, remembered him as naturally gifted in many different areas: 'Rio was one of those kids who was talented at everything. Even as a chorister he was a great singer. He also had a great talent for basketball. He was the best football player we had. He wasn't head and shoulders above the rest, but he was very determined and really applied himself.' Denise Winston was Rio's tutor at the school for five years. 'He was a bit of a Jack the Lad and at one stage he did seem to be falling in with the wrong crowd. But his mother was always there at the end of the phone and if he thought I was going to ring her he'd soon buck his ideas up.'

One of Rio's most daring late-night pastimes was to visit a friend in a nearby flat who had cable TV. They would stay up late to watch foreign league matches. 'We'd watch anything we could. A lot of European football especially. We were also bunging football videos on all the time. The player I really wanted to be like was Dutchman Frank Rijkaard. Not when he played at the back. He was a midfielder then.' One of Rio's favourite soccer videos was about the genius of George Best. He would make notes while watching it and then try to repeat some of Best's trickery out on the playground the following day.

Watching all that TV football simply reinforced Rio's determination to make it as a professional player. 'I wanted to play football, and fortunately I had the talent as well as the determination.' But there were other kids on the estate who wanted to earn big money and didn't care if that sucked them into a life of drugs and vice. 'I had a couple of friends in prison. It's unfortunate but it's part and parcel of life for some people brought up in certain environments.'

Janice knew she had to be vigilant and Rio has always been grateful. He said: 'My mum was really strong. She never let me off the estate unless she knew where I was. I had to tell her the time I would be back. We lived on the fourth floor of the flats and because the lift was always broken I always had to run up the stairs to tell her where I was off to.' Often, by the time Rio got back down, his mates were halfway along the road. 'But I knew that if I went off the estate without telling my mum I'd get a good seeing-to when I got back. It got on my nerves at the time, but I'm grateful now for the way she treated me.'

At Bluecoat, still greatly influenced by his father, Rio

showed an interest in drama as well as football. 'I always wanted to be the centre of attention. I loved singing, dancing, acting.' When he was 13 the school put on a performance of the musical Bugsy Malone and he was given the role of Fizzy, the man who swept up the floor of a speakeasy. It was Rio's first opportunity to sing on stage and he belted out a number called 'Tomorrow'. He explained: 'To me Fizzy was the top man and I had to sing that song. I couldn't wait.' He never forgot the standing ovation he got from the audience at the end of that night. 'It was wicked, wicked. That ovation just went on and on.'

Meanwhile, at the local league matches on Saturday and Sunday mornings, Rio was showing off a different kind of talent. Goodwin was astounded by the number of scouts who were turning up to watch Rio. It could only be a matter of time before one of them snapped him up.

3

When Rio was 14 something happened to one of his Bluecoat friends, which is still reverberating around Britain to this day. On 23 April 1993 a bunch of racist thugs murdered schoolboy Stephen Lawrence at a bus stop near his home in Eltham, south-east London. Rio recalled: 'The whole school came to a standstill when we were told. Stephen was three years older than me but we used to mess around together and have a laugh playing daft games on each other. It was a terrible shock when he died.'

As Rio vividly remembered: 'It was mad. The whole day got frozen. People were coming in saying, "Stephen Lawrence got stabbed." He was a quiet, nice boy, into art and music. He had a purpose and wanted to do something in life. For him to be taken away that way seemed so unreal. People didn't know what was going on, or why.'

There was a lot of anger among black students at Bluecoat. Some talked of taking revenge on the white youths suspected of involvement. But Rio knew that revenge would serve no real purpose. He diplomatically tried to encourage his seething school mates to calm down.

He knew from first-hand experience that violence would achieve nothing. He'd survived on the Friary Estate by treading a thin line between the good guys and the bad guys. There was no point in starting a race war. In the days following Stephen Lawrence's murder, Rio avidly read up about the lives of his two latest idols – Nelson Mandela and Martin Luther King. More than ever he wanted to understand where all this hatred came from.

By this time Goodwin was analysing matches for Middlesbrough manager Lennie Lawrence as well as being Blackheath and District Schools League organiser. He often went straight from Saturday-morning school games to watch senior matches, mostly in Division One to check out Boro's future opponents and before long he began taking Rio along with him. It was a great education for the youngster. 'Dave would tell me, "Watch him, he's a good player, and him too, look at the formation, see what they're doing at corners." So I got a bit of knowledge about the game, and that was really good for me.'

The first club to make a proper approach for Rio and persuade him to consider joining them was Queens Park Rangers. Rio trained for a few months at QPR but hated making the journey across the Thames to west London, so it always seemed unlikely he'd stay with the club. Middlesbrough whisked Rio up north to try and persuade the 14-year-old to sign for them. 'They wanted him as soon as they saw him,' Goodwin explained. 'But I sensed that Rio wouldn't be happy so far away from his family. So, even though I worked for Boro, I told him not to make his decision just for my sake.' Rio told Middlesbrough he wanted time to think over their offer.

Then Charlton made an approach to sign him. He went for a trial at the Valley but was so upset by a racist remark made by an opponent during the trial that he told friends he didn't want to join them. Next followed a chance to go to the FA's National School of Football Excellence at Lilleshall, in Shropshire, but again Goodwin believed the teenager wouldn't be able to handle being away from his family and London. There were even rumours that Millwall were about to make a grab for Rio, whose Peckham friend Tony McFarland had just been signed by the south-east London club.

West Ham heard about this talented kid in Peckham and asked him to attend a trial but he failed to turn up despite repeated requests. So one night coach Frank Lampard arrived unannounced at Rio's home and persuaded him that the Hammers really did mean business and that a YTS contract was on the cards if he proved a real talent. A few days later Rio travelled to east London for the first time in his life. Hammers' manager, Harry Redknapp, recalled: 'He never came to us as a kid with a big reputation. He had no England schoolboy honours or anything like that. Dave Goodwin was the scout who first told me about him. But Frank Lampard put in a lot of work to bring him to West Ham and it paid off.'

All the attention seemed to spur Rio on to produce even more impressive performances for the Blackheath and District Schools League. He was then given a try-out for the England U-15 squad. Afterwards he was handed an assessment that read: 'One pace. Lacks concentration. Good attitude. Mark: B.' His failure to get an 'A' and make the squad left Rio devastated.

Soon Rio's schooling at Bluecoat was being seriously affected by his training at West Ham. His teacher Angela Rezki explained: 'There were a few times when we clashed with West Ham because Rio would be fit enough to train with them and then tell me he was injured so he had to miss lessons. But he was never big-headed about it.'

Rio's hunger for football was growing by the day. He couldn't bear to be without a ball at his feet for more than a few minutes. He'd stand on his own on the edge of the playground on the estate practising tricks and improving his control. He was soon reading countless books about the game. One of his favourites was an autobiography by the legendary Jimmy Greaves. Rio gleaned lots of useful tips by reading it and it also helped him redefine his ambitions. Self-confessed alcoholic Greaves was full of dire warnings about drinking and getting consumed by the adulation of fans. 'I borrowed that book about Jimmy Greaves from the school library and learned all about what he suffered and what he put others through. It shocked me to see what could happen to someone who was such a major figure in the game,' Rio said.

4

One rain-lashed night Harry Redknapp climbed aboard the West Ham team coach, contemplating a grim five-hour journey back from Newcastle. After seeing the Hammers slump to defeat, their manager wasn't exactly in the best of moods. As the bus headed down the A1, he took a mobile call from his dad who had just got back from seeing West Ham's rookies pull off an amazing comeback against Chelsea to lift the Southern Junior Floodlit Cup. He was full of praise for one particular youngster.

'I've just seen the best kid I've ever seen play for your youth team.'

'Who?' replied Redknapp.

'Guess,' came the old man's response.

Redknapp recalled: 'I went through the names and when I couldn't guess who, he told me, "That young lad Rio Ferdinand."'

The young Hammers had lost the first leg 4–2 at Upton Park and few believed they stood any chance of winning the return by a big enough margin to take the trophy, but they did it. Rio was just 15 at the time and giving three years away to most of his opponents. But he looked the best player on the pitch, running 60 or 70 yards with the ball at his feet, showing pace and skill. Redknapp recalled: 'He was the sort of player English football had been crying out for – someone who could bring the ball out of defence with style and flair. He was a midfielder when he came to us and we converted him into a central defender. You look at all the greats and they have moved back there. Franz Beckenbauer, Lothar Matthaus ... they began in midfield and looked so cultured when they went to the back.'

Rio was on his way. He had a starring role in the Hammers' Youth Cup Final team in 1995 and even though they lost the final, the word was spreading fast that West Ham had a special kid on their hands. While most teenagers sat at home playing video games, Rio watched even more football tapes to improve his knowledge. And because he wanted to learn more about every aspect of the game, he also continued to go to matches with Goodwin.

On 1 August 1995 Rio signed his first playing contract with West Ham on the Upton Park pitch in front of a crowd of 25,000 waiting for the kick-off of the first Premiership game of the season. Janice was there to see the proud moment, and says: 'It was really emotional. I thought back to all those times we had been shopping for football boots.'

Rio signed with West Ham under their YTS which gave him a £35-a-week deal and meant he had to attend Kingsway College, in central London, on a part-time basis to do a course in Sports Science. Once he'd successfully completed the scheme at the age of 17, he would sign a professional contract. Goodwin sat in on Rio's full contract negotiations later that year when he signed a five-year professional deal with West Ham for £450 a week.

The 1995–6 season turned into a learning experience for Rio as he played regularly for the West Ham reserves and began to adjust to the faster pace and strength required for the adult game. At six feet two inches he was commanding in the air and strong on the ground. Some of the backroom staff were soon urging Redknapp to try Rio out, but he resisted the temptation for most of that season – until yet another injury crisis forced his hand and he had to put the teenager on the bench. Rio's first Premiership chance came as a substitute in the final game of the campaign, a 1–1 draw with Sheffield Wednesday. It was an occasion he would never forget. 'My first touch – the ball came over to me and bounced near the touchline. I just smashed it up to row Z of the stands and the crowd started cheering and laughing.'

Nobody, including Rio, remembers much more about his first-ever senior appearance for the Hammers. But within days of that first outing with the big boys, the teenager noticed reports in the national press suggesting that other Premiership sides were already interested in signing him. It was very distracting at first because his only aim had been to get into the first team and then consolidate his place.

There was another surprise when he was called up for the England U-21 squad along with team-mate Frank Lampard Jr, the son of the coach who had persuaded Rio to join the Hammers. The buzz on the football grapevine was that Rio was definitely one to watch. But it was clear he was going to have a tough time trying to break into the

West Ham first team, in which Redknapp's preferred back two central defenders were Croatian Slaven Bilic and Dane Marc Rieper.

At his home in May 1996 Rio picked up a letter and thought there had been a mistake. It was addressed to him but it was an itinerary for the full England squad's Euro '96 campaign. 'I'd only played one game for West Ham. I looked at the letter again and it was me they wanted. I ran round the house screaming my head off. I was making so much noise my mum came charging after me saying, "What's wrong? What's wrong?"'

England boss Terry Venables had invited Rio to join the squad to get a feel of the international scene. For three weeks the rookie defender lived with the squad, trained with the team and stayed in their hotel, absorbing tips from England's finest. 'Nervous? You bet,' he recalled. 'Have I got the ability? Or will I look out of place? And do you know what? As soon as I got out there and had my first touch it seemed perfectly normal.'

By August 1996 Rio and Lampard were pressing hard for Premiership places in the West Ham team. Redknapp was facing constant injury problems and must have been tempted to blood his two young starlets sooner rather than later. In the end he resisted the temptation but was confident enough to use them both as regular substitutes over the following few months. Rio was soon getting frustrated. 'Harry maybe thought I was a bit too young and a bit too eager at that stage. I was desperate to get in the first team. I let it get on top of me, thinking about it too much,' he recalled. Eventually Redknapp decided to ship him down to Third Division Bournemouth. It turned out to be an inspired move, which provided Rio with some essential first-team practice. He also got on extremely well with Bournemouth's veteran manager, Mel Machin.

Rio put in some good performances on the pitch but spending his nights in a £31-a-night hotel on half board was a miserable, lonely existence for a lively young Londoner. He was restless and homesick and even had to take his kit home after training every day and wash it. But, as the table showed, Bournemouth remained unbeaten when Rio played for them and Machin was soon raving about the teenager down the phone to Redknapp: 'Rio has got so much natural ability and is so quick that he could play anywhere. He went up front at times for us, but his best position is at the back,' Machin said.

Rio was just going into his third month with Bournemouth when he was recalled by Harry Redknapp because West Ham had injuries. Machin told his old pal Redknapp: 'Don't be frightened to stick him straight into the Premier League. You'll be pleasantly surprised how well he'll cope.'

5

Harry Redknapp hauled Rio back from Dorset at the end of January and plunged him straight into the sort of first-team action he'd been dreaming about for years. First up was the Hammers' tricky third-round FA Cup replay against Wrexham on 25 January 1997. It was certainly a baptism of fire and although Rio bedded well into the West Ham team, the result was a sickening 1–0 defeat. However, he had done well enough to be picked for the Hammers' next game.

Rio scored his first goal for West Ham at Blackburn the week after the FA Cup tie. That night he travelled back down south in the Hammers' coach and went straight round to his former coach's home. Dave Goodwin's wife, Kate, remembered: 'There was a knock on the door at 11.30 pm and it was Rio, grinning like a Cheshire cat. He said, "Please tell me you videoed the goal." Then he ran upstairs, put the video on and kept rewinding it, doing a running commentary, saying, "And he goes up and he shimmies around the ball, and it's a goal!" for about an hour.'

He wasn't the only one impressed by Rio's performance

and the goal. A few days later Manchester United boss Alex Ferguson called Redknapp and asked if Rio was for sale. The response was sharp and to the point: 'Sure, if we can have David Beckham.' The Hammers boss was keen to cool the hype surrounding his brilliant young defender. He said: 'We'll start talking about him playing for England after he's had 50 or 60 good games. I'm hoping he'll stay level-headed.' And Rio knew it was essential to keep learning his craft and listening to the experienced bunch of defenders around him like Slaven Bilic. 'Slaven played for Croatia in World Cup qualifiers and in the European Championships and played all over Europe. He was the bee's knees in my book,' Rio said.

Towards the tail end of the season West Ham offered Rio a new greatly improved five-year contract worth approximately £4,000 a week. His life was changing rapidly and his old Bluecoat pal Mark Atkinson never forgot the day Rio returned to his old school to hand out an award. 'Rio arrived in his BMW and I kept my Ford Fiesta parked around the back. I'm envious of all the money he's earning but I'm not jealous of him. I've bumped into Rio out and about. We have a chat and he's still got his feet on the ground.' It was typical of Rio to show up on his old manor and lend some support to his friends.

Going into the new season, Redknapp insisted that team spirit was at an all-time high. 'For the first time since I've been here, there's not a player at the club I would rather see the back of. When I started with Billy Bonds there were half a dozen who were a disgrace. Bill wanted them out, I wanted them out, but it takes time. Now everyone here wants to play for the club. The Premier League is the place to be. It's a very exciting time.'

There was already talk that Rio might develop quickly enough to be in England's World Cup squad the following year but that would mean impressing international boss Glenn Hoddle and before that, persuading Redknapp that he was worth a regular place in the Hammers' starting line-up. Rio played down his chances – 'It all sounds a bit far-fetched,' he said. 'It's nice to hear people say that kind of thing about yourself. But if you sit and drool over that, you could become obsessed. I don't let it get to me.' But, behind the scenes, his international stardom was already being plotted. His grandparents' nationalities meant he could have played for either Ireland or France, but he'd already made the crucial decision by turning out for the English U-21s. He later explained: 'I was born here, I'm from south London and my mum's English. Simple as that.'

Hoddle dispatched his assistant, John Gorman, to White Hart Lane to watch Rio's progress on the second Saturday of the 1997–8 season. The teenager's performance as sweeper during West Ham's 2–1 win over Tottenham was so superb it prompted some Spurs officials to describe him as the best young defender in the world. Even Gorman admitted: 'Rio's obviously a great prospect but I wouldn't like to put too much pressure on the lad. After all, he's only had two games this season, but we will be keeping close tabs on him over the coming months.'

Rio's feet were kept firmly on the ground by West Ham's assistant manager, Frank Burrows, who always picked the two nine-a-side teams during training. Redknapp later explained: 'The other day it was the "Good-looking" team against the "Uglies" and he picked Rio for the Ugly line-up. Rio couldn't believe it. All through the match, he kept muttering, "It's impossible", but it was a good laugh and he joined in with the spirit of the thing.'

There was certainly nothing ugly about Rio's performances. Simon Barnes in *The Times* wrote: 'At the age of 18 he is a trifle long in the tooth to be considered an infant, but he is a fine and precious talent. The point is not that he can play football, but the fact that he understands it. He understands the rhythms and the patterns, the well-laid strategies and the sudden inspirations that make up the game of football. He is a defender with ball skills, but that fact does him an injustice. A footballing centre-half is usually a big bloke who likes to fanny about on the ball and then gets caught out in some mad foray upfield. The point with Ferdinand is that there are no frills in his game. He eschews the easy back pass and turns forward neatly to lay the ball into midfield, but there is nothing self-indulgent about it.'

Out of the blue at the end of August, the scene was set for Rio to become the second-youngest player, after the legendary Duncan Edwards, ever to put on an England shirt. With Arsenal's Tony Adams and Martin Keown out and Stuart Pearce and Sol Campbell nursing injuries, Rio was called up for the England squad for the World Cup qualifying clash with Moldova in early September despite having just two U-21 caps and 16 Premiership starts to his name.

Everyone at West Ham tried to play down the situation because they wanted to ensure that Rio's transition from ghetto kid to international football star went smoothly. 'The kid's definitely got a lucky streak but you know what they say, "You make your own luck in this life"', said one who should know.

The problem was that Rio's luck was about to run out.

6

On 31 August 1997 Princess Diana and Dodi Fayed died when their chauffeur, Henri Paul, smashed a Mercedes into a concrete pillar in a Paris tunnel. Paul's decision to ignore basic rules about not drinking and driving helped deprive the world of one of its most glamorous figures.

A few hours after the Princess's death, in the early hours of the morning of Monday, 1 September, Rio was pulling out of a garage in his BMW in Colliers Wood, south London. His lights were off. He was stopped by the police and breathalysed and found to have 55 micrograms of alcohol per 100 millilitres of breath. He was just over the legal limit of 53 micrograms.

Rio told the police officers he had no idea alcohol was still in his system but that didn't stop them arresting him for drink-driving. He had gone out with a bunch of mates following the Hammers' thrilling 3–1 victory over Wimbledon two days earlier and also to celebrate his England call-up. They went out in his car, but returned in a taxi to his home in Peckham because he was worried he might be over the limit. But Rio then made the mistake of having three more drinks at dinner with friends on the Sunday evening before driving home in the early hours. This effectively 'topped up' the alcohol remaining in his blood.

Not surprisingly, news of Rio's arrest soon leaked out to the media but the nation was in such a numbed state after the death of Princess Diana that it didn't make the expected huge splash in the tabloids. That was Rio's only piece of good fortune that week. But the modest projection of the story didn't stop Fleet Street from asking the inevitable question: 'Will Rio still play for England against Moldova?' In the circumstances Glenn Hoddle had little choice but to say no. But he insisted Rio stay with the squad. 'I wanted him to see what he was missing out on,' the England boss said. 'This being his first call-up it had all the more impact. We have had a long chat. He's very disappointed with what he's done. He feels he let himself, his club and his family down. He's not out for good but if he goes and does something else in a month's time, then there's a problem.'

Three days later – on 4 September – Rio appeared at Wimbledon Magistrates Court, where he pleaded guilty to drink-driving and was fined £500 and banned from driving for a year. The day after his conviction, Rio issued a statement to the media in which he promised to pick up the pieces of his shattered career and even admitted: 'I've been so naive. I'm just so sorry. It's a harsh lesson for me to learn, being so close to gaining my first full England cap. I made a mistake for which I am dreadfully sorry. This will be a test of my character. I have to prove to people who have stood by me that I can bounce back.'

At the England training camp at Bisham Abbey, Hoddle

encouraged England stalwart Tony Adams to have a chat with Rio. As he later pointed out: 'It took Tony until he got to 30 to find the lesson that Rio has had now. It has to be good for the boy to speak to someone like Tony, who's been through it and can explain what it means.' Adams helped counsel Rio and showed a real concern that the teenager might fall victim to the sort of temptations that had once landed him in jail for drink-driving.

Rio did penance at Bisham Abbey while the rest of the squad prepared for the World Cup qualifying game against Moldova at Wembley and his chance to be his country's second-youngest player ever had been dashed. It was a cruel reminder to all up-and-coming young players about their future conduct. Hoddle left the door wide open for Rio when he said: 'I am not saying that he won't play for England in the future. He hasn't robbed a bank and he hasn't killed anyone but between Harry Redknapp and myself we will see how he reacts to what's happened.'

Only seven years earlier Redknapp had lost his best friend in a drink-driving accident. Now he found himself facing one of his brightest young protégés knowing that he had flouted the law. Redknapp was honest enough to acknowledge that knocking back a few lagers in the players' bar was seen as the professional norm but said: 'We must educate young players. Why should they want to get loads of drink down them when it leads to doing silly things and getting into trouble? Rio has been a silly boy, made a big mistake, and now must take his punishment. Glenn Hoddle has my 100 per cent support. Rio is basically a sensible boy and I am confident this will just be an unfortunate incident on his path to the top.'

Rio had learned his lesson. He had been the brightest star to emerge from Peckham – a place where few make it out of the ghetto – and he had the world at his feet. Now he knew that the only way to answer his critics was to go out there on the field and produce some even greater performances. But even that could be difficult.

On 24 September 1997 he received a severe lesson on the differences between the Hammers and the Premiership top three – Manchester United, Liverpool and Arsenal – when the Gunners thrashed West Ham 4–0 in a goal spree mainly inspired by that deadly Dutch duo Marc Overmars and Dennis Bergkamp. Unfortunately for young Rio, his marking of Bergkamp left a lot to be desired. Rio was left gasping by the magnificence of master marksman Bergkamp, only comforted by the thought that no defender in the world could live with the Dutch master in that form.

Three days later the Hammers were set to take on mighty Liverpool and everyone was talking about the expected clash between two of the country's most exciting young stars – Rio Ferdinand and Michael Owen. The pair had become friends at England U-21 level and Owen had made it clear he was determined to follow Rio into the full squad. The Hammers came out 2–1 winners over Liverpool and proved that Rio was far from demoralised by his recent troubles. He produced an awesome display of defensive play and skipper Steve Lomas said after the game: 'West Ham have always been accused of having a soft underbelly. Now each of us will get hurt for the team. We'll all go in, whereas maybe before others would have pulled out. We have pace in attack through Andy Impey and Stan Lazaridis, a big strong defence with Rio Ferdinand, David Unsworth and now Ian Pearce.'

Everyone at the game – including Hoddle – noticed how Rio effectively snuffed out master goal poacher Robbie Fowler, although he did have a tougher time against the pace of Owen. But when Liverpool pinned West Ham against the ropes during an exciting last 20 minutes, it was Rio who helped see them through for the three points. The *Daily Mirror* gushed after the game: 'Rio performed with such towering authority in front of Hoddle that if he is not given a reprieve it will prove only one thing – the England manager holds grudges.'

Two days later Hoddle was due to name his England squad for the make-or-break qualifier against Italy in Rome on 11 October. He concluded Rio wasn't quite yet ready to face the mighty Italians but his World Cup dreams might still be realised because England earned a creditable 0–0 draw and were guaranteed qualification to the finals.

The Hammers' next Premiership game against Newcastle looked as if it might prove a testing time for Rio. But Redknapp believed that his young star defender was up to the test. 'I haven't lost any sleep over Tino Asprilla,' he said, referring to the Magpies' Colombian striker. 'He's a terrific player, has a lot of talent and I've a lot of time for him. But young Ferdinand is a tremendous player. And with David Unsworth and Ian Pearce there as well, I'm sure we'll cope'

As it turned out, Rio put in a Gladiator-style display in the clash with Newcastle. By the time the second half came around, he was so full of confidence that he started forcing play into the opposition's half. When England hardman

David Batty and a couple of fellow Geordie defenders came swinging their boots in his direction, he managed to leave them all kicking at thin air. The Geordies squeezed out a miraculous 1–0 victory, but Rio's talent was undeniable as he produced a display that made the cocky Colombian Asprilla look like a Sunday-morning park player. Many West Ham fans came away that afternoon saying that Rio would captain England one day, just like another great Hammer, World Cup winning skipper Bobby Moore.

It was clear that the Bobby Moore tag could turn into a millstone around Rio's neck if he wasn't careful. Rio had been studying videos featuring some of Moore's greatest performances. 'Recently I saw clips of him in action. He just glided forward, didn't he? And that tackle he made on Jairzinho in the 1970 World Cup, well, from what everyone tells me, that epitomised him.'

In the end Rio's international career was always going to thrive because Hoddle wanted to play with a sweeper and he believed the West Ham defender had the capability to perform that special role. Rio was determined to succeed but knew he could still improve every aspect of his game. 'Talking and organisation are things I need to improve,' he said. 'If you're playing in the centre, you've got to be a good talker or lead by example. I'd like to be able to do both. Tony Adams is a fine example and Alvin Martin when I first went to West Ham was brilliant at it.'

7

In November 1997, less than a year after suffering all alone in that miserable boarding house in Bournemouth, Rio found himself once again a member of Glenn Hoddle's World Cup plans, relaxing in the luxury of the England headquarters – a £110-a-night hotel in Hertfordshire with breakfast an extra tenner. This time he'd been promised a definite slot on the subs' bench against fellow World Cup qualifiers Cameroon at Wembley.

Rio cast his mind back to those days on the south coast and said: 'I grew up – I had to. Bournemouth was one of the best things that ever happened to me.' Now it was time for the next stage in his learning curve. The game against Cameroon was even more significant for Rio after his drink-driving arrest. It meant he'd been forgiven and he fully intended to repay those who'd shown such loyalty to him.

He admitted a perfectly understandable attack of nerves. 'I've kept a video collection since I was very young and studied all the great players. Suddenly I looked around the dressing room and there was Paul Gascoigne, Paul Ince and

Sol Campbell, the players I've watched for the last few years and I was among them. I asked myself if I was good enough to be there and then realised if I wasn't, I wouldn't have been picked in the first place. I've always had confidence in my ability but when I was younger I certainly didn't think this sort of thing would happen so quickly.'

As he warmed up in front of the Wembley crowd he couldn't help but feel emotional. And that was before he heard yells from the fans. 'I'd thought nobody really knew me at that stage but "Rio, Rio" was ringing around Wembley. I was thinking, Whoa, what's goin' on here?'

Rio came on in the 40th minute for the injured Gareth Southgate and looked at home almost immediately. He drew loud cheers from the crowd for one penetrating move that almost led to a goal. As he later recalled: 'I thought to myself, Go out there and enjoy the game. Didn't I just! It has given me a taste of international football, and now I want more.' There were aspects of the night that Rio would never forget for the rest of his life. 'First of all, the national anthem. That's a massive experience. Standing there and listening to it gave me the shivers. Next, running on to the pitch as sub and Paul Ince slapping me on the back. Then getting the ball from Andy Hinchcliffe was a big thing – my first touch in international football. Best of all, perhaps, was a run I made through the middle. I brought the ball out of defence and played a couple of passes, and if Robbie Fowler had played it back to me I might have scored. Instead, when I put him through he had a shot. That run did a lot for my confidence. The crowd were shouting my name, and that makes you realise how good it is to be on the international stage.'   England won 2–0, and after the game Hoddle was full of praise for his young debutant, saying: 'He did nothing wrong, everything right.'

When Rio got home that night he watched a video of the game and criticised every mistake he made by making a note of it on a piece of paper. 'You have to do that to improve,' he later explained.

Rio's next ambition was to start a match for the national side. He reckoned he still had a realistic chance of going to the 1998 World Cup Finals in France. By now he had learned that he couldn't constantly be looking over his shoulder worrying about others being picked ahead of him.

In December 1997 Manchester United boss Alex Ferguson once again tried to sign Rio. This time he proposed an unusual pay-now-play-later deal in secret talks between Hammers and Old Trafford bosses. Under the agreement, Rio would be allowed to stay at West Ham for another two years before moving to Man United. Alex Ferguson had already had a £6 million bid for Rio knocked back. West Ham told the Premiership holders they'd have to pay at least £10 million to land the youngster. 'Ferguson had been keeping an eye on Rio ever since he turned out for Bournemouth. He was like a man obsessed and determined to get his man in the end,' one Man United source later explained.

West Ham later denied there had ever been any proposed deal. Harry Redknapp hit back furiously, saying: 'It's a load of rubbish. If we were even thinking of selling Rio then we don't deserve to be in the Premiership.' But behind the scenes, there was no doubt that Man United were putting West Ham under immense pressure to sell the youngster and they were prepared to try and pull off any type of deal to get their man.

As usual, West Ham's dilemma was that they were desperately in need of the cash to keep the club afloat. But was Redknapp really prepared to sell their best prospect since Bobby Moore? In the end the east London club decided they would hold on to their 'investment' for the time being. It was too soon to sell him and, in any case, they knew his value would rocket over the coming couple of years. It didn't make business sense to sell him – yet.

No one thought it was a coincidence that Rio signed a long-term contract with West Ham just days after the Man United stories surfaced in the press. The Hammers knew they didn't stand a chance of hanging on to the talented defender in the long term, but at least they'd get a king's ransom when the time finally came to cash in their chips. Rio's new deal was worth around £2.5 million over seven years, according to newspaper reports. Not bad for a teenager who'd been on a £35-a-week YTS wage three years earlier and was only on £400 a week when he made his debut for the Hammers the previous year.

Rio's most painful reminder of his recent slip from grace was not being allowed to drive a car until the following September. In some ways his 'house arrest' suited the powers that be at Upton Park and England because it meant he couldn't get out much. But living on one of the worst council estates in Europe didn't exactly fit the image of being a well-paid football star and a lot of those 'bad influences' remained on his doorstep. Many in both camps were hoping that when Rio did get his licence back he'd settle down with a nice girl, buy himself a flat and become a responsible adult. Others had their doubts and were already calling him a 'Spice Boy' with delusions of grandeur.

However, his recent conviction emphasised to Rio that he needed to hold on to the most solid base in his life – his family, especially his mum Janice. So he took her and her painter-and-decorator husband Peter St. Fort, along with his brothers Anton, 13, Jeremiah, two, and his eight-year-old sister Sian to see a plush new house miles away from the Friary Estate. His mum recalled: 'Rio was pushing me into all the rooms, saying, "Go on, Mum, have it, have it." I didn't even know where we were. Peter and I had been looking for a house in Peckham but Rio ended up taking me to this house in Mottingham.' Tucked away in a suburb on the borders of south-east London and Kent, the property had five bedrooms and a garden. It was ideal. Rio picked up his mobile and called the estate agents to tell them that he wanted to buy the house within minutes of them all looking at it. 'She's having it,' he said.

Rio also kept in close contact with his dad, whom he described to one pal as his 'best friend'. Somehow, despite the painful parting between Rio's mother and father all those years earlier, Julian had continued to be a big influence on his life. 'Julian was and still is a good father. He's always been there when Rio needed him, offering good sensible advice and never expecting anything in return,' says one close family friend.

On the financial front, Rio was determined not to squander the millions of pounds that now seemed certain to come his way. He had an accountant to make sure he made some wise investments rather than spending it all at once. 'I knew that if I had it all sitting there in one account I'd probably spend the lot. My huge weakness is clothes.

When I went out Christmas shopping to buy things for my family I came back with things for myself.'

In February 1998 Rio's big mate Michael Owen was called up for his first full England cap against Chile at Wembley. The night before, Rio was swallowing his disappointment by playing for the England 'B' side at West Bromwich Albion's ground. But, typically, he put in a sterling performance to show the coaches he still deserved to be selected for the senior side and by early spring he genuinely believed that he was back to his best form in the lead-up to that summer's World Cup in France. He'd had a few poor games a couple of months earlier, but now he had a realistic chance of going to the biggest football tournament in the world even though he'd only been used as a substitute, coming on late in the World Cup warm-up against Belgium.

There was a nervous wait until May when Hoddle chose his final squad of 22 players for France. Rio was one of them. He walked back to his room at the England hotel in Hertfordshire, sat down on the edge of the bed and found himself engulfed in a full range of emotions. For a while he couldn't utter a word. Then came a breathless excitement at what it all meant to him and his family, and he made an ecstatic call home to break the news. 'When Glenn said simply that I was in, it was the most unbelievable feeling. I had been champing at the bit, nervous, expectant, not knowing what to think.'

After his family, he called up his team-mate Frank Lampard to tell him that he wouldn't be taking a planned two-week holiday in the sun after all. And Harry Redknapp, Rio's ever-loyal boss, said: 'Everyone is talking about Rio going along for the ride and experience, but if he gets the chance in the World Cup he's going to be a permanent fixture. Getting selected for the squad is a marvellous tonic for the lad and it's wonderful for West Ham too. It's been a long time since those three West Ham greats, Moore, Hurst and Peters, helped England win the World Cup but if Rio keeps maturing as I believe he will he could be right up there with them too. Rio is going to get enormous experience over the next month and it's going to help West Ham in the Premiership next season.'

8

Although Rio had squeezed into England's World Cup squad, in the end he didn't make an appearance. England's eventual defeat against Argentina in France left the nation in a state of depression over the failure to progress any further than the last 16. But many observers believed that with up-and-coming young players like Rio waiting in the wings things could only get better.

At West Ham's Chadwell Heath training ground, Harry Redknapp continued to be blown away by the youngster's extraordinary natural talent. The Hammers' boss explained: 'We used to do these one-on-ones, where the attacker would face one defender as he went in on goal. Eyal Berkovic said to me once, "I've been here two years and it's a waste of time if you get Rio. I've never seen him beaten." It was true. Even Paolo Di Canio would try all his tricks, but then make a move and Rio would nick the ball away from him.'

At the beginning of the new season striker Ian Wright signed from Arsenal, and there was a feeling at Upton Park that great things lay ahead for the east Londoners. So-called hardman Neil 'Razor' Ruddock, who'd arrived from Liverpool for a bargain-basement £750,000, and Chilean international and World Cup defender Javier Margas were added to join Rio in defence. Seasoned campaigner Ruddock would prove to be Rio's most important guiding light. Razor was a tough, blunt Londoner with a strong heart and a no-nonsense approach to the game. Rio, the graceful young apprentice with superb ball control and an uncanny ability to dribble and to dummy opponents, could not have been more different.

However, Ruddock soon influenced Rio's play on the field. He later explained: 'I think my experience over 13 years helped Rio. I just told him to keep talking, keep talking. Even if you're saying rubbish, just keep talking because it helps concentration and others around you. Rio even helps me now.' Later Rio acknowledged that he learned a lot from his new team-mate and some at West Ham say to this day that Razor's toughness rubbed off on the teenager and helped his game develop in a different direction. Ruddock taught Rio how to give as good as he got and that, more than anything, helped the younger player to establish himself in the West Ham team during the campaign.

Rio knew that the current season was crucial to his development as a player because there had undoubtedly been a few occasions where he'd definitely come off second best. 'Putting that right is something I have to sort out in my head,' he said. 'I have to be right physically and mentally. The World Cup was a great experience even if I didn't play and my goal for the season is to start getting into the England team as a regular. I know that'll need hard work and dedication. But first and foremost I've got to get things right for West Ham. If I don't, then nothing else will follow.'

A couple of weeks later all Rio's plans were shattered by a leg injury which meant he had to pull out of the England squad for the European Championship qualifier in Sweden. But Redknapp was still convinced his young defender had a big future at international level. 'He will be the best defender in Europe by the time the European Championship Finals are staged in 2000,' he said. 'Rio is ready for England now. He's outstanding but he's nowhere near his peak.'

The buzz on Rio's footballing ability was growing by the day. His 20th birthday, on 7 November 1998, was marked by a superb article in *The Times* by Oliver Holt who wrote: 'Ferdinand is one of the few genuine creative defenders to have emerged in this country in the past 20 years, a player who is much, much more than a stopper. He can defend with the best of them – as he showed in his shackling of Alan Shearer during West Ham's 3–0 victory over Newcastle at St James's Park last Saturday – but he also has a great gift for turning defence into attack.'

Rio recovered from injury and received his England call-up for the friendly against Czechoslovakia. England won 2–0, although Rio almost conceded a goal in the dying minutes when he gave away possession and only a fine save from Nigel Martyn rescued him. He was making progress with England but was disappointed when in February 1999 he heard Hoddle had been sacked following an interview in *The Times* in which he was alleged to have said disabled people suffered because of 'Karma'. The remarks caused public outrage and even prompted Prime Minister Tony Blair to voice disapproval. Step forward Kevin Keegan, seen by many as the man to save the England team and bring some more heart and soul into the job after the technical obsessions of master craftsman Hoddle. The only problem was that Keegan was no great fan of Rio Ferdinand. Having moved forward so fast, Rio now faced a new battle to try and establish himself in the England team under a new boss. It wasn't going to be easy.

That summer, the rumour mill connecting Rio to a host of big football clubs started up all over again. A lot of the speculation had been sparked by his protracted negotiations with West Ham about an additional clause in his contract that gave him an automatic ten per cent cut of any future transfer fee. Rio's agent Pini Zahavi knew only too well that West Ham would one day be forced to sell and the player wanted to be certain he'd get his cut.

A party of Italians, headed by Roma's chairman, Franco Sensi, were rumoured to be on the way to London to start negotiations and that started a ripple effect among other big European clubs. Real Madrid were reported to be about to make a £12-million bid, and others were waiting and watching developments. Meanwhile West Ham's chairman, Terence Brown, continued to refuse Rio's demand for ten per cent of any future transfer deals. Rio mischievously fuelled some of the speculation about his possible departure to Italy by joining a radio interview with his Hammers colleague Paolo Di Canio at West Ham's training ground. Taking the microphone from his team-mate, he told Italian listeners: 'I know the Olympic Stadium in Rome and I know it is a beautiful city. Roma fans are exceptional. I hope we will see each other soon.'

Despite Kevin Keegan's reservations about Rio's footballing talents, the youngster re-emerged as a shock candidate for a place in the England team to face Scotland in the European Championship 2000 qualifier at Wembley. He only made it on to the subs' bench in the end, but at least Keegan considered him, which was encouraging. England lost 1–0 but went through to the European Championship after thrashing the Scots at Hampden Park in the first leg.

With his driving licence now back in his wallet and a luxurious brand-new penthouse flat in London's upmarket Docklands, it wasn't surprising that Rio's skills off the field started to get tongues wagging. In the autumn of 1999 he went on a series of dates with blonde Spice Girl Emma Bunton. But Rio had problems coping with Emma's fame. 'Rio just couldn't handle all the attention she got,' one of his oldest friends said. 'Rio comes from a family where the mother is the one who runs things. In some ways, he felt that his girlfriend's role was to keep out of the spotlight, not attract even more attention than he did!'

The football critics began circling Rio because he'd endured a torrid time on the pitch over a six-week period in the autumn of 1999 thanks to a series of uncharacteristic errors while on duty for West Ham. There was a dreadful mistake at Anfield which allowed Liverpool to snatch victory. That was preceded by numerous blunders against Sunderland, Leicester, Aston Villa and, in Europe, against the French side Metz, all of which raised serious doubts about Rio's reputed £12-million price tag. He also found himself back in the England U-21 side for the first time in more than two years for a match against Yugoslavia in a play-off for the chance to be at that summer's U-21 European Championship. Rio shrugged off his apparent 'demotion' by Keegan to prove he was still a very talented footballer, especially at that level, as England won 3–0.

Rio's new riches had given him a Jaguar XK8, designer clothes and a penchant for London nightclubs. But he still believed his football was heading in the right direction and he refused to let the 'Keegan problem' make him downcast. He even saw his return to the U-21 team as the chance to confound his critics and prove he was still worthy of a place in Keegan's senior squad for Euro 2000.

Behind the scenes, though, Rio was growing restless about something else – the lack of silverware at West Ham. He admitted to one reporter: 'I do get a bit jealous when I see others challenging for trophies and I've made no secret that I want to move abroad one day to develop as a footballer and broaden my horizons as a person.'

But the latest newspaper gossip linked him not with a move abroad but north where Leeds United were now leading the chase for his services. Once again Redknapp was quick to pour scorn on the story: 'David O'Leary has £20 million to spend in the summer and he wants to give me £7.5 million for Rio Ferdinand. But the day we sell Rio and our other young players is the day when this club starts to die. People talk about Sol Campbell, but Rio is a better player than him. He has made a few mistakes, but he is such a special player. He'll be an international for the next 10 years. I have no doubt. And he should certainly be part of England's European Championship squad.' Then a fresh round of rumours circulated that Rio was on the verge of signing for Leeds in a £15-million deal. A typically blunt Harry Redknapp instantly hit back: 'I'm sick to death of hearing that Rio's on his way to Leeds. It just isn't going to happen.'

Meanwhile many were speculating that Rio would make England's 22-man squad for Euro 2000 despite Kevin Keegan's reservations. But Rio didn't make it in the end. Many football commentators were shocked by the England boss's decision, and one wrote: 'It seems appalling that someone with Ferdinand's ability will be left at home this summer.'

Instead Rio, Frank Lampard and Newcastle's Kieron Dyer, plus Leeds players Jonathan Woodgate and Michael Duberry, headed for the five-star Grecian Bay resort in the popular resort of Ayia Napa, in Cyprus, for a well-deserved summer break. Their antics with booze and girls shocked other holidaymakers and before long Rio's name was splashed all over the tabloids once again. It seemed he had learned nothing from his earlier lessons.

Back in London, there was bitter disappointment about Rio's behaviour in Ayia Napa. While he could be forgiven for the drink-driving offence since he was only 18 at the time, the same could not be said for this latest episode. Even the normally relaxed Harry Redknapp was infuriated by the behaviour of Rio and Lampard. He told one reporter: 'I spoke to Rio. I've told him that he has to be careful. He knows he was in the wrong.' He was at a crossroads.

9

Rio admits that being snubbed by Kevin Keegan for Euro 2000 was the crunch point in his career and was probably the making of him. 'I'd begun to think I was invincible, to get complacent with my game and I didn't prepare for matches properly. I fully expected to be picked for the team and, when I wasn't, I think it made me take stock.'

Others things also helped Rio 'take stock', as he put it; such as the fact that most other people were not as well off as him. He'd been particularly touched to get a letter from a 14-year-old boy in Ghana. 'He sent a photo of himself. He was really poor, with holes in his boots and a raggy kit. He wrote that he had posters of me all over his bedroom wall. He had looked around the world for a player to give him pointers on his game – and plumped for me. I thought, Wow, this kid's all the way from Ghana and I'm his idol.'

Rio knew the fast-approaching 2000–1 Premiership season could prove a watershed for him and he admitted: 'Every season is a big one for me, but I want to get the most out of it. Now it's time for some hard graft. I want to get down to the nitty-gritty. It's time my football did the talking.'

Deep down he knew that unless he left West Ham his England career might well run out of steam. Not being in the Euro 2000 squad confirmed his worst fears and it was a devastating blow to his pride and confidence. Kevin Keegan's decision was a wake-up call for the young defender. It didn't matter how much talent he had; unless it was properly used and carefully developed, then his career could plunge into free-fall. And his behaviour in Cyprus hadn't done his standing much good, either.

Rio had good reason to be worried. Perhaps a move to Leeds would help him get away from all those bad influences in London. He could ask for no better a tutor than the boss at Elland Road, David O'Leary. The Irishman wouldn't stand for any of the indiscipline that was tolerated at West Ham and he'd probably give Rio a few harsh lessons. Rio was realistic enough to know the time was approaching when he had to escape the unhealthy influences on his life.

Harry Redknapp and Hammers chairman Terry Brown knew the day would eventually come when Rio would leave Upton Park but for the moment they wanted to hang on to their young investment. Rio's value seemed to be escalating by the month and at this rate he would probably be worth something like £20 million by the end of the season. But in November 2000 Rio took a call from the Hammers' managing director, Paul Aldridge, which would change the course of his life. The club was seriously considering an £18-million offer for him from Leeds United. 'It was a big turning point in my life,' Rio recalled. 'There was a lot of speculation, and West Ham were saying they weren't going to sell me, but then I got that call. I was shocked because I hadn't asked to leave but then I thought, if they want to sell me, then I'm going to go. When I heard the size of the fee I thought, bloody hell, or something stronger.'

Leeds' chairman Peter Ridsdale flew to London and booked into the plush Conrad Hotel at Chelsea Harbour then caught a taxi to meet Rio's agent Pini Zahavi at the Langham Hotel in central London. Half an hour later Rio turned up and introduced Ridsdale to his mother, who wanted reassurance about how life up north would be for her son. Rio later recalled of his meeting with Ridsdale: 'Five minutes with their chairman and my mind was made up. The key was that I was talking to people whose ambition matched mine. If my family was okay about the move, it was going to happen. Mum and Dad said to me, "Whatever you're happy with, we'll be 100 per cent behind you," which is the way it's been all my life.'

Rio finally signed on the dotted line for Leeds United before watching his new team-mates beat Arsenal 1–0 at Elland Road. At a packed press conference before the match, he explained the reasons behind his move: 'I am very pleased to be joining such an ambitious club. The manager's ideas here at Leeds played a big part in me moving here. I saw the squad here, which also had a big effect. I appreciate what West Ham have done for me, although this is a new chapter in my career. Hopefully my career can now start going again. The fee involved doesn't concern me. I'm here to play football.'

Rio was hailed at Leeds as the new messiah – the final piece in O'Leary's jigsaw, which would enable the club to mount a serious challenge for European and domestic honours. The Leeds players had all been impressed by Rio's awesome display a couple of weeks before his transfer when West Ham beat Leeds 1–0 at Elland Road. O'Leary saw Rio and fellow central defender Jonathan Woodgate as the lynchpins of the team.

The day after Rio committed his future to Leeds United 10-year-old Damilola Taylor was murdered while he walked home through the very same estate where Rio grew up. Rio heard the news from a bunch of mates, who hit the phones within hours of the brutal killing of the Nigerian schoolboy. Rio later recalled: 'I thought to myself, Bloody hell, what is going on there? I was brought up a couple of minutes from where Damilola was killed and because you're from there you want to get involved in some way, to get people to sit up and listen.'

Within days of the murder – which made headlines across the world – Rio was asked if he'd help by presenting a TV appeal for information which might help catch the killers. The interview was filmed at his new club's training centre at Thorp Arch, and he was given a set of scripted answers beforehand. He glanced down at the answers, carefully folded the piece of paper up and put it to one side. 'You ask the questions,' he told the interviewer. 'I'll be okay.' What followed were a lot of highly emotional, unscripted answers that seemed to get to the core of the problem. They were delivered with an earnestness that made people sit up and take notice back in south-east London.

Rio took the Damilola murder to heart. He explained: 'I love Peckham. It's, like, my place. When I was young and went to school outside Peckham I made sure everyone knew where I was from. I know my life now is a long way from all that, but I can still remember what it's like to want things and to walk down to the shops and wish you had what's in them.'

Rio turned up on his old manor and took a group of journalists on a tour of the estate, where he soon found himself listening to kids airing their views on subjects that were very similar to what he experienced as a youngster. Children complained of being harassed for money, being threatened verbally and physically. Rio even heard that in the weeks before Damilola's murder many of the kids on the Friary Estate witnessed a build-up of problems from certain gangs of youths but residents were too scared to tell the police. Just like Rio many years earlier, most of them had concluded that the police did not care about them because they were black. Many youngsters said that even if they were in trouble they would never ask a white policeman for help.

Rio had two cousins who attended the Oliver Goldsmith School, where Damilola had been a pupil. 'It's a terrible tragedy and the nation has been forced to wake up to what's happening in places like this because of such a horrible, horrible incident,' he told reporters as they toured the estate. But deep down, Rio knew there was nothing new about the Damilola tragedy and he even admitted to the journalists: 'It would be absolutely awful if people believed this was just a one-off incident.' He had seen many examples of this when he was a kid.

10

Rio's career at Leeds could not have got off to a worse start with the team on the receiving end of a 3–1 thrashing by Leicester at Filbert Street and he admitted he wondered if he'd made the right move, but said: 'Then I went training with the lads and the anxieties started to ease. I could see I was among some of the best players in the country. I knew I was in the right place.'

Rio moved into a new house in Wetherby, near Leeds' training ground, together with his 2,000-plus collection of CDs, which were to be given a room of their own. He missed his mum, brothers and sisters but Janice travelled up north to look after Rio at least once a month. And he insisted he was now more interested in playing computer games than chasing girls. He claimed to be virtually unbeatable on a PlayStation.

Rio remained deeply concerned by the lack of arrests in the Damilola Taylor case. He even made a fresh appeal in newspapers: 'It would be nice if whoever did it came forward or if somebody would drop the police a line and let them know who the killers are. It won't bring young

Damilola back, but it would help his family to come to terms with what has happened.' He feared that Damilola's murder would make people treat places like the Friary Estate as virtual war zones. 'I don't want Peckham to be abandoned,' he said.

The murder spurred Rio on to get even more involved in the problems of inner cities. He was determined to give something back. In the rundown Chapeltown area of Leeds he helped launch a cybercafé for underprivileged children. He also joined RABS – the Revolutionary And Breaking Stereotypes football academy, which encouraged kids in Leeds to grow in confidence.

On the football front, the appointment in autumn 2000 of Sven-Goran Eriksson as England's first foreign coach was of major importance to Rio because he knew the Swede was a long-time admirer of his skills. The Swede was very different from Hoddle and Keegan, who'd walked out after a disastrous home defeat by Germany in a World Cup qualifying-round game. Eriksson exuded calmness and was even nicknamed by the Italian press 'the rubber wall' because when manager of Lazio he soaked up everything they threw at him so softly and then bounced back a gentle answer.

Not only had Eriksson heard plenty of praise about Rio, but he had a soft spot for Leeds United after visiting their training camp as a would-be coach more than 20 years previously. And, to cap it all, Leeds were to play his club Lazio in the Champions League on 5 December. Eriksson was working out his notice after Lazio had struck a deal with FA bosses that he would not join England until later the following summer. That game would have been the perfect stage for Rio to show Sven what he was made of except that he wasn't eligible for the Champions League until the following February, when the second stage began.

Leeds impressively beat Lazio 1–0 in Italy, which, ironically, forced Eriksson to conclude that 'working out his notice' at the Italian club was not a very practical idea. Within weeks he'd joined the England set-up full time.

Now happily settled at Leeds, Rio was hoping the next stage of his career plan – a regular place in the full England team – would soon follow. He knew only too well there were no guarantees of a full England place with the likes of Wes Brown, Gareth Southgate, Sol Campbell and Martin Keown around but he was determined to push hard for selection. 'I made a lot of mistakes when I was younger,' he admitted. 'They were well documented but I now think they were a blessing in disguise. I didn't realise I was so much in the spotlight. I will make other mistakes but I have learned from the ones I have already made. People shell out a lot of money to see you play and you have got to behave in a responsible way. That was hard to grasp at first, but you eventually get there.'

Rio's first appearance in the Champions League was on 13 February at Elland Road against Anderlecht in the second stage. Leeds won 2–1 and a week later thrashed the Belgians 4–1 away. Rio was then called up for a starting place in England's back four in the 3–0 friendly defeat of Spain. He looked strong and confident alongside Sol Campbell. England's new boss seemed determined to give youth a chance, which was great news for Rio and the other up-and-coming young players.

Behind the scenes, he had been working hard at

developing his game to that of a flat back four, which was very different from the approach at West Ham. By the time the Champions League quarter-finals began he seemed to have adjusted his game superbly. He was also handed the captain's armband in the absence of regular skipper Lucas Radebe and relished the responsibility.

Within days, Sven-Goran Eriksson was hailing Rio as an England captain of the near future. 'I'm delighted to be honest,' Rio said. 'As a kid you dream about leading your team out and this is a chance to take with both hands because to be captain of such a huge club is something to be very proud of. This sets me up for the season, knowing the manager and the staff think I am capable of doing the job. As I have always said, I came here to win things and if that happens as captain then that will be fantastic.'

The emphatic 3–0 victory against Deportivo La Coruña in the first leg of the quarter-finals looked certain to secure Leeds a highly unlikely place in the competition's last four. But what made Rio's day more than anything else was that he scored one of the goals. Irishman Ian Harte crowned an impressive evening with a classic assist when goalkeeper Valerón could only flick his 65th-minute corner into the path of Rio for his first-ever goal for Leeds and his first scored in nearly four years. Leeds lost the second leg 2–0 at Deportivo in front of a hostile 35,000 crowd and just scraped through to the semi-final 3–2 on aggregate. Uncharacteristically, Rio got himself booked for kicking the ball away in frustration in the 23rd minute. This followed a tussle with Fran as Leeds seemed to be crumbling under incredible pressure from the Spaniards.

Leeds hung on grimly during the last quarter of an hour as Deportivo battled in vain to score a third goal that would have equalled the aggregate score.

In *Only Fools and Horses*, Peckham's most famous fictional hero, Del Boy, constantly accentuates the positive. 'He who dares, Rodney. He who dares wins.' So it seemed that Del Boy and Rio had another thing in common besides hailing from Peckham. Del always dreamed of the day he'd make it big, and Rio was determined to be the best defender in Europe while still barely out of his teens.

Rio's goal against Deportivo La Coruña, followed by one against his former club West Ham and then one against Liverpool, brought his tally to three in five matches – all this for a player who hadn't scored in years.

Rio's family and friends continued to pop up north to see him. The move to a quieter community seemed to have helped him to keep more level-headed. And his settled state of mind at Leeds was about to help turn him into an England regular. He appreciated the gentle art of persuasion practised by Eriksson, saying: 'He's clear and concise with his instructions on how he wants us to play. The coach has created an atmosphere already in which no player can afford to assume he's too good to be dropped. And I don't see that situation changing. I've played for managers who shout a lot. Not this one. He'll let you sit there and quieten down before he starts talking. Then he'll tell you what he wants in a calm, composed manner.' That spring, England squeezed out a 2–1 victory over fellow World Cup group members Finland. Rio and Sol looked uncomfortable at the back, with Rio even going missing at the corner that resulted in Finland's goal.

The build-up to the Champions League semi-final against Valencia was to prove a vital experience for Rio. Leeds had been the underdogs of the tournament since getting through the pre-qualifying rounds the previous summer. They also had to cope with a torrent of negative publicity generated by the approaching court case involving Lee Bowyer and Jonathan Woodgate over an assault on student Sarfra Najeib.

The first-leg semi-final at Elland Road was played in light rain and Valencia controlled the first half, although Rio stood firm and gave an impressive performance. In the second half Leeds came close to scoring on a number of occasions, but a 0–0 draw on home soil meant all the odds were stacked against them for the return leg the following week. Back in Spain, Valencia proved too strong for Leeds as Juan Sánchez struck twice and Gaizka Mendieta fired a third to give them an emphatic 3–0 victory in front of a partisan crowd of 53,000. For Leeds, the misery was completed when teenage striker Alan Smith was sent off in the last minute for a tough challenge on the French World Cup winner Didier Deschamps. Defeat was a sad ending to Rio's European adventure, but he and his Leeds teammates had done the team proud.

The young child that would become one of the footballing sensations of his era.

Above: Rio's mother Janice outside the playground of the Peckham school where Rio learned his passion for football.

Below left: Rio's birth certificate.

Below right: The family together – Rio with mum Janice, brother Anton and sister Sian.

Above: Rio in the Blackheath Bluecoats Secondary School team photo. Rio is second from the right in the front row. At the right-hand side of the middle row is Leon Simms, still Rio's best mate who hangs out with him whenever he comes to London.

Below: Rio in his district football team, back row, third from left.

Top: The Peckham estate where Rio was brought up. It is on this estate that young Damilola Taylor (*below left*) lost his life. Rio spent his time secretly trying to track down Damilola's killers, and he was also shocked by the death of his close friend Stephen Lawrence (*below right*).

Rebecca Ellison – Rio's glamorous wife.

Above and below right: The man in action, and (*below left*) celebrating his sensational goal against Denmark in the 2002 World Cup with Goldenballs David Beckham himself...

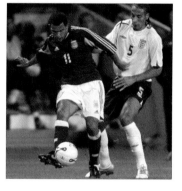

Above: Rio at the West London hotel where in March 2004 his appeal against an 8-month ban for a missed drugs test was dismissed by an independent 3-man panel.

Below left: In January 2005, Rio showed his altruistic side when he joined the Stand Up Speak Up anti-racism initiative.

Below right: Rio Ferdinand harries Argentina's Carlos Tejez during the England 3-2 win in November 2005, which raised even higher hopes for England success in the 2006 World Cup.

Stylish and contemplative – who knows what the future holds for the world's finest defender?

11

That summer Rio had a night out at that popular watering-hole the Epping Forest Country Club and met an attractive brunette called Rebecca Ellison. She was softly spoken and made no attempt to flutter her eyelashes at Rio, but he was hooked from the moment he first caught sight of her. This time, thought Rio, I'm going to take it one step at a time. He courted Rebecca in an old-fashioned manner until he felt confident that she was genuinely interested in him. Then he persuaded her to stay at his house in Wetherby. Rebecca wasn't interested in going out clubbing and Rio liked that. He always responded better when the women he met were happy to stay out of the limelight.

Rio's career had received the double boost of a highly publicised run in the Champions League plus confirmation from Sven-Goran Eriksson that he saw him as a regular team member. And by the summer of 2001 Rio knew more or less for certain that his seat was booked for the 2002 World Cup Finals in Korea and Japan if England managed to qualify.

But he already had a nagging feeling in the back of his

head that Leeds weren't really up there with the very top clubs. It could be one of the main reasons why they never won anything. He then got quite upset when Leeds chairman Peter Ridsdale stated publicly that Frank Lampard was not worth the £11 million Chelsea paid for him in a recent transfer. In Rio's book that seemed an unnecessary insult and it was the first time he felt things were happening at Leeds of which he did not completely approve.

Next up for England was the mammoth task of facing the Germans in Munich to try to salvage any hope of qualifying for the World Cup Finals. Rio would be making his eleventh start and winning his 16th cap, Eriksson had given the entire squad a new confidence in their abilities but now it was time to justify it on the pitch. And they did so, thrashing their old rival 5–1. The opposition were completely destroyed even though they went one up after just six minutes. The opening half-hour was fast and furious as both sides missed numerous chances. Then Owen scored a hat-trick, which, along with goals from Heskey and Gerrard, sealed the Germans' fate and put England back in control of World Cup Group 9. The historic victory was without doubt the greatest moment in Rio's international career to date. He looked commanding at the back. It was Germany's worst home loss in nearly 70 years and one that made the rest of the footballing world sit up and take notice of Eriksson's gifted pack of young lions.

But as so often with young sides, they almost threw away all the good work in the next match at Old Trafford. It looked set to end in disaster until David Beckham curled in a stunning free kick in stoppage time to grab a 2–2 draw. England had qualified for Korea–Japan 2002. Meanwhile, the Germans' 0–0 draw with Finland left them with the tricky task of playing home and away to Russia in order to qualify for Korea–Japan 2002.

After brief celebrations, it was back to reality for Rio as Leeds beat Grasshopper 2–1 in a UEFA Cup tie. The match came hot on the heels of five successive defeats for Leeds on the road in Europe, plus a first League defeat at the hands of lowly Sunderland the previous weekend.

During the 2001–2 Premiership season, Rio devoted large amounts of time and effort to improving the prospects of youngsters whose future appeared as bleak as his own had once seemed. Already an accomplished and confident public speaker, he became a regular visitor to schools in London and Yorkshire, where he addressed racial issues and tried to encourage youngsters to work their way out of the ghetto.

Rio also became deeply involved in the Prince's Trust and the National Literacy Trust, whose director, Neil McClelland, was impressed by his enthusiasm. At Christmas 2001 Rio persuaded Leeds to stage a dinner at which players were to paint designs on plates for a Prince's Trust charity auction. The team had just crashed to an appalling defeat at bottom-of-the-table Leicester, but Rio cajoled his dispirited team-mates into a spot of artwork and in the process raised £25,000.

But much of the good work being done by players like Rio was overshadowed by a court case involving two of his Leeds team-mates. Many cynics believed that the trial of Jonathan Woodgate and Lee Bowyer was proof that the saying 'British justice is the best money can buy' was spot on. The two millionaire players walked out of court as free men after an Asian, Sarfraz Najeib, was left battered, bleeding and unconscious in Leeds city centre. One of Woodgate's friends was found guilty of the attack and sentenced to six years.

Woodgate, described by one witness as having jumped on the victim, though clearly the jury didn't believe it, was convicted of affray and the judge sentenced him to 100 hours of community service. Bowyer, though blood had been found on his jacket and the judge accused him of telling a series of lies under police investigation, was cleared of all charges. However, because of those lies, the judge imposed on Bowyer the obligation to pay £1 million in costs. Woodgate would also have to pay the same amount.

The FA Cup third-round tie between Cardiff and Leeds at Ninian Park in January 2002 proved yet another turning point in Rio's career. The game itself was a disaster for the Premiership side, but, more importantly, it ended in scenes of crowd trouble that shocked the footballing establishment. And for Leeds boss David O'Leary the 1–0 defeat was the moment when his career at Elland Road began to slide backwards. The result was a disaster for Leeds' season and Rio was starting to wonder how much longer he could stay at a club that promised so much but delivered so little.

Following that controversial FA Cup defeat against Cardiff, Rio joined a long list of Leeds players needing treatment for injuries. He was told he'd definitely miss the top-of-the-table clash with Newcastle plus a home clash with Arsenal the following Sunday. But he was hopeful he might recover in time to face Chelsea and Liverpool.

On 3 February 2002 Leeds intended to teach a few

lessons to the mighty Liverpool, who were suffering from a dreadful loss of form which had resulted in nine consecutive winless League games. But Leeds were smashed 4–0 at Elland Road and looked dejected as they left the pitch. Having led the Premiership at the turn of the year, they now seemed to be in free-fall. And to make matters even worse for Rio, he put the ball into his own net for one of Liverpool's goals.

When Leeds were knocked out of the UEFA Cup by Feyenoord in the fourth round, the team seemed to be suffering from the biggest loss of form since O'Leary had taken over from George Graham nearly four years earlier. But there was one statistic Rio had good reason to be proud of: by the end of February 2002 he had not been booked for an astonishing 76 League games. He explained this away by pointing out that he preferred to show his skills than his studs to opponents.

12

Off the pitch, Rio had finally matured into a genuine role model. He was the principal organiser of Leeds United's £50,000 sponsorship of 10 runners, whose hard-sweated earnings would be shared between the Outward Bound Trust and the Damilola Taylor Trust. 'I have tried to do as much as possible for the Damilola charity,' he said, adding, as he'd sought to emphasise often before, 'but this kind of tragedy has been happening for a long time on the streets where I was brought up. Not always incidents of kids dying, admittedly, but certainly kids getting stabbed and people getting shot. It is not a nice thing to say but that has all been part and parcel of living down there. Damilola's death has simply put it under more scrutiny. Now action, money and Government intervention is needed.'

Then came the shock news that two teenage brothers accused of Damilola's murder had been acquitted on all charges, including murder, manslaughter and assault with intent to rob. The court's decision left the boy's parents and many on the Friary Estate deeply shocked. Rio made another visit to Peckham just after the Old Bailey decision and was angered to find that many of the old problems had returned with a vengeance, despite a period of calm following the murder.

Rio's work in the community was acknowledged when the local council granted him the Freedom of the Borough of Southwark. Meanwhile the 'other' Rio still managed to find time to enjoy the good things in life. He now lived with Rebecca in one of the smartest villages in Yorkshire and ferried himself to training in the snug-fit cockpit of a brand-new £120,000 dark-blue Ferrari. He also owned a top-of-the-range Jaguar and a Range Rover and dined at the best restaurants. He wore even more designer clothes, Gucci t-shirts, Victor Victoria cargo pants, discreetly accessorised with a Patrick Cox Wannabe belt, and of course a hefty gold Rolex on his wrist. It was all such a far cry from those humble beginnings in Peckham.

Leeds lost 1–0 to Fulham on 20 April, which killed off any hopes of the club qualifying for the Champions League. Their season was basically over. Thank goodness Rio still had the World Cup to look forward to. His place in the squad for the 2002 World Cup was already assured as he'd been in all Eriksson's England teams to date. But there were some other genuine surprises when the 23-man group was announced in May. Included were midfielders Joe Cole of West Ham and Owen Hargreaves of Bayern Munich. With typical understatement, Eriksson told reporters: 'We have some difficult matches but an extremely exciting time ahead of us.'

Just before the squad departed for Japan, Eriksson told Rio that he would lead the team in the World Cup Finals if David Beckham didn't return to fitness in time following his much-publicised foot injury. The England manager believed that Rio had already proved his leadership qualities while skippering Leeds.

As the England squad arrived at their base camp in the Far East, stories about Rio leaving Leeds started to surface in the UK and he admitted to the *Sun*: 'You are always flattered when big clubs are interested in you.' The club in question was undoubtedly Manchester United and they'd already tabled a £20 million offer. Leeds' financial problems and their failure to qualify for the following season's Champions League ensured that the big boys were now circling the club like vultures. Rio refused to comment any further but back in England it was rumoured that Alex Ferguson was about to up the offer to £25 million. With five days to go until the start of the World Cup, it was then reported that £30 million was now on the table. Throughout the world of football there was astonishment. Was any defender really worth that sort of money? And had Leeds decided that if they could virtually double what they'd paid for Rio just 18 months earlier then the deal would be green-lighted despite the damage it might do to their future? Rio – with four years on his contract still remaining – was understood to have a quick-release clause and all the time, in the middle of all this, was a deeply unhappy O'Leary, well aware that his most talented player could be about to leave the club.

In football they say that Alex Ferguson always gets his man in the end so the charm offensive that the club put into action after the England squad arrived in the Far East for the 2002 World Cup was no surprise. David Beckham, Paul Scholes, Nicky Butt and Wes Brown all urged Rio to join them in the quest for more trophies the following season. As the squad carried out their final preparations on the Korean island of Jeju, Rio talked to family, close friends and associates back in London, including his powerful agent Pini Zahavi, who'd been on first-name terms with Ferguson for years. Then, in the middle of all this, Rio heard that David O'Leary had suddenly quit Leeds. Many believed his decision had been caused by the club's refusal to guarantee the manager that they wouldn't sell their star defender.

Rio's first-ever game in the World Cup Finals on 2 June proved a bitter disappointment for England, who were extremely lucky to escape with a 1–1 draw. They started well against Sweden, but in the second half were ripped apart by a well-organised side. Rio's biggest contribution came when he put a header over the bar from a David Beckham corner in the 37th minute. He also unintentionally unsighted keeper David Seaman when Andersson scored the equaliser for Sweden at 58 minutes.

The next match – against Argentina – was hyped to the hilt with all the usual emotional baggage of the 1982 Falklands War plus Diego Maradona's 'Hand of God' goal that helped knock England out of the 1986 World Cup and David Beckham's infamous red card in Argentina's penalty-shootout victory at France '98. A draw would be creditable, but a victory would probably secure England's passage into the next round as group winners. That would mean avoiding France and gave a clearer route towards the semi-finals. The dream win came true for Rio with a 1–0 victory. A Beckham penalty late in the first half was enough to do it. Rio and defensive partner Sol Campbell performed superbly. England were suddenly hailed as potential winners of the World Cup.

Rio had paid for his mum and his brothers and sister to fly out to Japan for England's 'group of death' clash with Argentina, and there Janice met up with Rio's dad, Julian. She recalled: 'We must have looked quite a sight. All of us were sitting in a line in the stadium wearing England shirts. We were just like any other supporters, except our kit had "Rio" written on it. Sian had her face painted red and white and she was draped in an England flag bibbing a horn. Every time he got the ball, we'd all shout, "Re-Oh! Re-Oh!"'

Rio was hailed as England's best player during the 0–0 draw with Nigeria. He showed great authority and on at least two occasions intercepted Nigerian attackers with superb skill and tenacity. Both teams were exhausted by the early-afternoon heat. Man of the match Rio told a packed press conference afterwards: 'We came here to get out of the group and now we have done it we want to go as far as possible.'

Back in England, newspapers were still having a field day about all the clubs allegedly lining up to try and buy Rio. They dubbed him 'the world's most wanted defender'.

England cruised into the World Cup quarter-finals with an emphatic 3–0 victory over Denmark and Rio was involved in the opening goal. His header from David Beckham's corner was off target, but Danish goalkeeper Sorenson knocked the ball off his own chest and over the line. Later FIFA awarded the goal to Rio. It was the perfect start for England, and a nightmare for Denmark, who even while singing their national anthem had looked nervous. After the match, Rio admitted it was a lucky scramble that led to his goal. 'My first thought was, What a rubbish header. I should have headed it in without the keeper touching it. Fortunately, it went in off him and there's no better feeling than scoring your first goal for England.' Goals by Heskey and Owen sealed the victory and after the game Rio even kept hold of his England shirt despite the fact that everyone else swapped theirs with the Danes. 'No way was I going to lose my shirt from a match where I scored,' he later explained.

Rio's favourite team after England was Brazil, so to have the South Americans as quarter-final opponents was a dream come true. 'Everyone knows how much I love Brazil and meeting them will be wicked. Ronaldo looks back to his best and I love to see a player like that doing well. When he is fit there is no one better in the world,' Rio said.

England's hopes of going all the way to the final were crushed by a brilliant footballing display by the Brazilians, who came out 2–1 winners. England scored first through Owen, but then Rivaldo got one back just before half-time and England were soon up against the ropes. In the second half, Ronaldinho's clever free kick completely fooled Seaman, and Rio and his team-mates never even looked like getting back into the game. They even failed to cash in when Brazil were down to 10 men after Ronaldinho was sent off in the 56th minute for a foul on Mills. With just over 10 minutes to go Rio was dispatched into attack as another striker in a desperate attempt to claw back a goal. But it was all to no avail.

At least Rio walked away with two mementoes from that final England game: the shirts of Rivaldo and Roberto Carlos, which he gave to his brother Anton after the match.

As Rio later explained: 'I got Rivaldo's shirt myself and then Roberto Carlos asked for mine, so I swapped another one with him. It's really something when a player of his stature comes looking for my shirt.'

So England were out of the tournament. Down but certainly not disgraced. And Rio emerged with an even bigger, worldwide reputation.

13

Rio had a lot of thinking to do on his return from the World Cup. The previous season at Leeds had definitely not gone according to plan. They'd won nothing, failed to qualify for the Champions League and were still haunted by the Bowyer and Woodgate court case. Then they'd sacked their manager. Rio reckoned the club had made a complete hash of handling the media. The low point came with the publication of David O'Leary's book *Leeds United on Trial*, which opened the club up to scrutiny when it least needed it.

In order to escape the intense media attention, he set off with England pal Wes Brown, of Manchester United, for a sunshine break in the gambling capital of the world, Las Vegas. Brown's presence ensured that Rio would be kept carefully informed of Alex Ferguson's quest to sign him.

On Monday, 24 June Man United's chief executive, Peter Kenyon, told the club's official website he'd spoken to his Leeds counterpart, Peter Ridsdale, about signing Rio and said: 'Over the next few weeks things will start to develop but there is nothing at the minute. At this stage Ferdinand is not for sale.' Leeds knew the defender's value had rocketed because he'd performed so superbly on the world stage but they were also rumoured to be £30 million in debt and desperate to sell some players in order to balance their books.

Rio wholeheartedly approved when he heard that Terry Venables was to be the new manager at Leeds. He felt he owed the former England manager for letting him join the Euro '96 squad when he was no more than a kid. He respected Venables immensely and he was looking forward to hearing what the cockney coach had planned for Leeds and a meeting was set up at a London hotel. Venables insisted Leeds was still the right place for Rio to continue his footballing education. But as Rio later explained: 'Mr Venables never asked me to say whether I would be staying or not. But I couldn't have given him an answer there and then because there was a lot to think about and I'm sure he understood that. As a person and a coach he's up there among the best of them. He said the sort of things I expected and you can see he wants to do well. This is his chance to stamp his mark on a club and he wants to do everything to make it a big success.'

On 14 July Rio rolled up at his mum's house in Mottingham in his brand-new £168,000 Aston Martin. He wanted the family to help him decide whether he should join Man United. Rio listened avidly to Janice as she explained the importance of loyalty. He heard Julian talk about the need to keep his feet firmly on the ground no matter how many millions of pounds were thrown at him. He even talked to his kid brother Anton about how it might all affect him. Anton was a very similar character to Rio and was now following in his footsteps at West Ham.

Newspapers claimed that bidding for Rio had opened at £28 million. Ridsdale still insisted he'd rejected his captain's written transfer request but behind the scenes, the deal was virtually complete. Pini Zahavi was confident that Rio would be playing for United when the Premiership opened in early August. 'He would be happy to join Manchester United,' he said. 'He wants to play in a bigger and better club and he wants to play in the Champions League.'

By 20 July there was total deadlock between Leeds and Man United over Rio's value but significantly when the Leeds party boarded a plane for a pre-season tour of the Far East, Rio was not on board. Sure enough, three days later he completed his move to Manchester United for an astounding £33 million. Ferguson had finally got his man and Leeds had got a healthy profit of £16 million over just 18 months.

Rio – now on a new wage packet of more than £60,000 a week – announced the transfer at a packed Old Trafford press conference and cited the ambition of Man United's England stars to win more medals as a major factor in his decision to move. 'I've seen the boys with England and they are as hungry as ever,' he explained. 'They said it's like they have not won a championship yet and they want to do so again. When you are with England, the United boys stay after training and work on little things. They are the players that are at the top and that is something I want. To be able to say I have played alongside the best and the hungriest players around is important to me.'

Rio admitted to the assembled press pack that he knew his move was a bold step – especially because of the fierce rivalry between the two teams. 'I made a decision to come here, as I thought it was a step on the way to improving me as a player. It wasn't an easy decision. I spoke to my family about loyalty. But at the end of the day, it is a short career and opportunities like this don't come around all the time.'

Also at the press conference on that day was Rio's girlfriend Rebecca Ellison, his mum and young sister. It was Rebecca's first real taste of the public spotlight as the lover of the world's most expensive defender. She looked calm and serene throughout the media gathering and made a point of watching proceedings from the back of the hall at Old Trafford. Then the couple went off house hunting in Cheshire's stockbroker belt.

Not everyone was impressed by Rio's move. The *Daily Mirror* published a story showing the similarities between what Rio said when he left West Ham on 27 November 2000 and what he said on leaving Leeds on 22 July 2002 under the headline 'NEW CLUB ... SAME OLD CLAPTRAP'

Rio had left Leeds because he was made an offer he knew he couldn't refuse. Man United remained the most glamorous club in the world and he knew he could win the biggest prizes at Old Trafford. He was concerned what Leeds fans would think and saddened when the supporters cancelled their Player of the Year presentation to prevent Rio collecting the award.

Having made the decision, Rio now had to concentrate 100 per cent on doing the business for his new club. The move to Manchester United was intended to address the weakness at the back of the defence that had contributed to nine League defeats the previous season. It had certainly convinced Frenchman Laurent Blanc, who said: 'My desire to win things at Manchester United is one of the reasons why I decided to come back to play one more year and I'm looking forward to playing alongside Rio, who is an outstanding player for his age.'

Just a few days after arriving at Old Trafford, Rio persuaded Ferguson to let him make his debut against Bournemouth in a friendly testimonial to their manager Mel Machin. All eyes were on Rio from the minute he stepped out to warm up with his team-mates at Dean's Court and this otherwise insignificant pre-season friendly was even beamed live on MUTV across the world, with China among the countries transmitting the match. A global audience of around 60 million was believed to have tuned into Rio's Man United debut.

Rio told the after-match press conference: 'It was great to get out there and I really enjoyed myself. I'm relieved I got that one out of the way. I am now looking forward to the challenge ahead. But this is Mel's day. He deserves all the praise in the world. He did a lot for me when I was at Bournemouth all those years ago, and I really wanted to come out and join everyone in paying tribute to him.'

Clearly, Rio and his agent had come out the real winners from his transfer to Manchester United. He was on a salary of more than £60,000 a week, putting him up there with the club's top names, including David Beckham. His five-year contract also granted him ownership of his image rights, allowing him to negotiate lucrative commercial deals. Then there was the small matter of the £3.3 million the club had agreed to pay to cover a pension contribution to the Professional Footballers Association, plus a payment of the agents' fees.

With his massive increase in wealth, Rio splashed out

£190,000 on a Bentley GT Coupe to match the tastes of David Beckham. Some at Old Trafford immediately dubbed the new team-mates the Bentley Boys. With a £110,000 Ferrari and that £168,000 Aston Martin already in the driveway, plus a two-seater Mercedes sports car and a 4x4 Escapade, Rio still went for the Bentley, a brand-new model not even in the showrooms yet. Rio put down a £50,000 deposit to make sure he got one of the first off the production line. Rio was told to expect delivery of the car, complete with white leather seats, walnut dashboard, DVD player and mini-TV screens, by mid-winter of 2002. By that time he hoped to have settled in a Cheshire mansion. Local estate agents were already on the lookout for a property with a pool, gym, snooker room and jacuzzi.

But despite the high salary, flashy motors and beautiful brunette Rebecca on his arm, it wasn't all smooth sailing. Rio received at least 10 death threats in the days following his transfer to Man United. Senior officials at the Professional Footballers Association were alerted, as well as the police. Two meaty ex-SAS bodyguards were immediately assigned to protect Rio whenever he was at the club's training ground or Old Trafford. One source at the club explained: 'Rio usually just shrugs this stuff off – but these letters are more sinister. They have gone too far.'

A security guard was also posted at Rio's mum's house in Mottingham because of taunts made in the street to members of the family. As he told his friend: 'Now that does bother me. They're havin' a dig at my family and that's completely out of order.'

14

Typically, Alex Ferguson was soon issuing a warning to Rio and any others who might think they would be automatically selected. 'It's simple. If players perform, they'll go in. If they don't, they won't. Performance is everything. You can't go beyond that. Reputations don't matter. I'm the manager of the biggest club in the world, with the biggest support base in the world, and my loyalty is to them. I've also got loyalty to the players, obviously, but the bottom line is I've got to produce a winning team. That's where decision making comes into it. I've been given that job and I've never shirked it. You might think it's hard, the players might think it's hard. but it's not. I remember that this club went 26 years without winning the League and since then things have changed around here.'

Rio didn't even fly out with Man United for their next pre-season friendly against Norwegian side Valarengen. Alex Ferguson believed it better for him to stay behind in England and then link up with the squad for a four-team tournament in Amsterdam the following weekend. Rio's full debut for Man United ended in a 2–1 defeat by Ajax.

He made way for his close pal Wes Brown in the 58th minute but Ferguson insisted he was pleased with his performance: 'Rio looked assured at the back. He read the game well and I'm happy with him.'

Dutch ace Ronald Koeman – now Ajax coach – was not so impressed: 'It's a bit too early to call him world-class. You are only that when you have proved yourself over a number of years at the highest level. The whole attention will be on him and everything will be analysed. It's not every player who can handle that extra pressure. Some so-called quality players can't handle the life and expectancy of being at a big club.'

For Man United's friendly with Parma in that tournament, Rio partnered John O'Shea in defence, with Roy Keane on the bench and David Beckham taking over as captain even though regular stand-in skipper Ryan Giggs was in the side. Heavy rain was accompanied by loud claps of thunder, and with the stadium roof open, the players found themselves sloshing around in the mud. United took the lead in the 23rd minute with a stunning move featuring some wonderful interplay between Veron, Rio and Beckham before Butt spread the ball wide on the right to the advancing Brown. He beat one defender and then whipped in a low cross, which was steered home by the left foot of Giggs. Minutes later Rio managed a deft feint on the ball before bursting off on the left wing to create space from which he picked out Solskjaer for a speculative overhead kick that stunned the Italians. United eventually coasted home 3–0.

On 10 August Rio wrenched his left ankle after 23 minutes of United's 2–0 win over Boca Juniors, leaving

Alex Ferguson without his £33 million centre-back for at least two weeks. Rio would definitely miss the first leg of the following week's Champions League qualifier against Zalaegerszegi in Hungary and he was unlikely to play in United's first two Premiership matches.

Meanwhile Rio's interest in acting had turned into a serious hobby. After taking those secret acting lessons while at Leeds, he was delighted to be offered a part in the second series of ITV's *Footballers' Wives*. Back in the real world Rio missed United's first two Premiership games, home to West Brom and away to Chelsea, through injury but he finally made his competitive debut for Man United in their second-leg Champions League qualifier at Old Trafford against Zalaegerszegi on Tuesday 27 August. Trailing by 1–0 after a late goal by the Hungarians in the first leg, United were undoubtedly facing their most important match of the new season. If they didn't progress into the Champions League proper, it could cost the club as much as £40 million in lost revenue. As it turned out, the opposition were thrashed 5–0, but Rio looked far from comfortable at the back of the defence. Halfway through the second half he made a terrible blunder, giving the ball away in front of his own goal, but was saved by a superb tackle by Blanc. Shortly afterwards Ferguson took Rio off and he was given ice treatment on a swollen ankle although many in the crowd wondered if he had been substituted before any more disasters occurred.

Rio produced a solid display for England in their 1–1 draw with Portugal in a friendly at Villa Park when England's goal was scored by Rio's former Leeds team-mate Alan Smith. The game was somewhat overshadowed by the inclusion in the England squad of Lee Bowyer and Jonathan Woodgate after their two-and-half-year ban because of the Leeds assault case.

But the most significant event happened a few hours after the game. Rio couldn't resist motoring down the M1 from Villa Park for a night out in London's sleazy Soho. He arrived at the trendy Sugar Reef bar with five friends and later a terrifying brawl broke out in the middle of the club involving some of the player's friends. Rio disappeared into the night minutes after the trouble flared up but it seemed that despite all the pledges and the 'calming influence' of Rebecca, Rio still couldn't resist the lure of the bright lights of his home city.

Rio's first big test of character on the pitch came the following Saturday, when Man United travelled to Elland Road for an important Premiership clash. They lost 1–0 to Leeds, but their defeat couldn't in any way be blamed on Rio, who gave a faultless display, despite non-stop heckling from the crowd. The names didn't seem to worry him, although he did appear slightly edgy on the ball. More hurtful was the fact that many pundits at the ground came away applauding Woodgate's performance at the heart of the Leeds defence. As Matt Lawton wrote in the *Daily Mail*: 'Of the two defenders Woodgate was by far the superior on an afternoon that proved a touch traumatic for the former Leeds captain.'

But the question on everyone's lips following United's second defeat of the season, which left them tenth in the Premiership, was whether the Old Trafford bubble had burst. After five matches the team had managed its worst ever start to the Premiership. And those who assumed the arrival of Rio would see Ferguson's side return to the top of the League already appeared to be very much mistaken.

United's Premiership title bid had got off to a rocky start with a run of injuries and mixed results. Initially, they excelled in the Champions League but failed on the domestic front. But their league challenge firmly got back on track with a victory over Liverpool at Anfield with Diego Forlan scoring both goals in a 2–1 win. In December 2002, United also managed impressive victories against Arsenal and Newcastle United. In the Champions League, they beat Juventus both home and away and were undefeated in the Premiership.

Rio's old West Ham mentor, Harry Redknapp, revealed that the only Manchester United player he'd select for his own side would be his former young player Rio. By now the Portsmouth manager, Redknapp made his comments on the eve of his side's third round FA Cup defeat at Old Trafford in January 2003. 'Man U have got many outstanding players but Rio is extra special. Yet he was never really an outstanding talent as a kid.'

The new year also saw United reach the Worthington Cup Final. However, United's Champions League campaign came to an end in the quarter-finals when they went out to Real Madrid. But confirmation that Rio's decision to move to Manchester United had been correct came when the club clinched the Premiership with 83 points. As Rio joyfully held aloft the Premiership trophy at the end of the campaign he must have reflected on what a good decision he had made because his former clubs Leeds and West Ham struggled to survive in the Premiership.

He had every reason to be delighted but critics were quick to point out that United's unsuccessful European adventure undoubtedly exposed the fact that Rio was still far from the finished article. Onetime Leeds and Man U favourite Johnny Giles wrote a highly critical article headlined 'THE TWO Rs EXPOSE HUGE GAPS IN RIO'S KNOWLEDGE OF DEFENDING' in which he claimed that Ferguson could not avoid asking some awkward questions about his £33 million investment's performances at the back. 'Rio at 24 is young enough, but the worry is that a big part of a defender's performance will always be not so much technique as attitude of mind. Watching Ferdinand, you sometimes have to wonder if he has the potential to develop that defender's instinct and mindset. Part of his problem is that all footballers have a tendency to become creatures of habit and, in the Premiership, this can be a major problem when someone like Ferdinand, who in an average league game looks quite masterful, has to step up his effort against players of the quality of Raul and Ronaldo.'

During United's two quarter-final games against Real Madrid it had certainly been true that Rio sometimes looked as if he was lost in a minefield and, undoubtedly, Ferguson had noticed his shortcomings on the European stage. Now people inside football were asking for the first time if Rio could really make it in the big time. Could he acquire the kind of nerve and timing that distinguished the outstanding defenders?

Giles added, 'Ferdinand's worry now must be that his boss, who has made clear his priority of winning another European Cup, has seen enough to add another name to his shopping list. A name like John Terry, a player who long ago proved he didn't need to be told that the main role of a defender is to defend. Ferdinand needs to grasp that truth as a matter of urgency. His United career will, sooner rather than later, depend on it.'

Rio's activities off the pitch also continued to hit the headlines and tarnish his reputation. In June 2003, he was 'exposed' by the *News of the World* when two hotel workers alleged he attacked and humiliated them during the England team's 'training break' prior to a crucial Euro 2004 qualifying game against Slovakia. The incident took place at the luxurious Hyatt Regency hotel in southern Spain's La Manga holiday complex. Chelsea's John Terry was also alleged to have been present during the incident. Neither of the alleged 'victims' would talk about the incident afterwards but one other worker at the hotel later told reporters: 'It was the talk of the hotel. The England team tried to hush it up and hotel managers ordered us not to talk about it to anyone, but by then it was too late.'

Rio needed an exploratory operation on a knee injury, which meant he would miss England's 2–1 win over Slovakia in a European Championship qualifier. He admitted: 'It can be quite depressing. We have the best surgeons, but you're still on tenterhooks before an operation as to how it'll turn out. It's best to get away if you can. I've had a few injury problems and never felt able to get into a proper rhythm. I'm really disappointed I won't be able to play at the moment but I will be rooting for the boys and I'm sure they will do the business.'

In the early autumn of 2003, yet more problems on the personal front emerged when the *Daily Mail* headline claimed: 'Party animal on the brink of ruin at 24.' It was an exaggerated story based on association and more than anything Rio had done but there was much worse to come. Rio was about to find himself at the centre of the biggest crisis of his headline-hitting career...

15

On 6 October 2003 it was publicly revealed that Rio had failed to take a routine drugs test at Manchester United's training ground two weeks earlier. He was immediately dropped from England's crucial match against Turkey and his international boss Sven-Goran Eriksson was said to be 'disappointed'. England needed to win or draw the Turkey game in order to qualify for the following summer's European Championships in Portugal and Rio had established himself as a valuable member of the team. He would be missed in defence.

Rio insisted to FA investigators that he was so preoccupied with moving house that he simply forgot to make himself available for the test, although he did provide a clear sample 36 hours later. However, his failure to attend when required remained a technical breach of the sport's strict anti-drugs code. Newspapers also pointed out that the delay in taking the test would have allowed some drugs, including recreational substances, to have passed through Rio's body and become undetectable.

However, Manchester United insisted they would stand

by their record signing and they immediately issued a statement: 'The player has not been charged with any offence, but has been asked to attend a personal interview to explain the reasons behind his non-attendance.' Rio undoubtedly faced an anxious wait until then.

Rio's agent and father-figure Pini Zahavi reportedly said the FA would be 'shooting themselves in the foot' if they banned him from playing in the Turkey game. Meanwhile the whole of British sport, not to mention the Government, was watching carefully to see how football's governing body would handle the delicate situation. The public and many newspapers were outraged at Rio's alleged 'forgetfulness' and Fleet Street let fly in typical fashion. A *Daily Mail* headline read: 'Treachery – pampered playboys betrayed our trust.' The paper's respected sports journalist Jeff Powell wasn't just referring to Rio but other England players who had stunned the FA by threatening to strike over Rio's 'suspension' from the game against Turkey. Powell wrote: 'Our man, Rio, they object, has been let down. So has our £30 million centre half, squealed his mighty club. So has our Mr Ferdinand, protests their shop-steward-in-chief (Gary Neville), the highest paid shop-steward-in-chief, the highest paid trade union leader in the land. And yes, Master Ferdinand has been let down. By himself.'

In reality, Gary Neville's attempt to rally the England players in protest against what they saw as kangaroo court justice against Rio was well intentioned, but the problem was that it actually highlighted the details behind the drugs test incident, which sparked even more questions about Rio's motivations. In the end, the England players' protest ran out of steam but Rio, the man at the centre of all the

controversy, continued to insist he was nothing more than an innocent man. Streetwise Rio knew the rules of the game and as far as he was concerned he had done nothing wrong.

But if he was hoping the scandal would calm down after a few days of tabloid outrage, he was to be bitterly disappointed. By the following weekend, the Sunday papers had also joined in and they'd uncovered some fascinating background information. The *Sunday Telegraph* revealed that at the previous World Cup in Korea and Japan, Rio had willingly provided a urine sample for a drugs test in a FIFA television broadcast aimed at educating the public about the importance of doping control. His willingness to co-operate with the film made Rio's failure to do the same at Manchester United's training ground all the more bewildering. It also proved that he was far from naïve when it came to providing samples to drug testers. Unfortunately for Rio, this particular story did nothing to help convince the world of his innocence.

At the *Sunday Times*, journalists provided their readers with a day-by-day, blow-by-blow account of the 'drugs test fiasco' as it was now being referred to. It emerged that Rio was told he had one hour to report for the drugs test after a three-man testing team arrived at United's Carrington training ground at 11.15 am on Tuesday, 23 September. Several players including Rio, Nicky Butt and Ryan Giggs were amongst those to be tested. United doctor Mike Stone even sent a reminder down to Rio while he was getting changed. United later insisted that by the time Stone realised Rio had forgotten to attend the drugs test, he had already left the ground. Meanwhile the testers continued waiting for Rio.

It was only after the testers left the training ground that United realised there really was a problem. The club then sent a number of text messages and voicemail messages to Rio's mobile phone but were unable to contact him. A club official claimed that Rio kept his phone switched off much of the time because of hate messages from Leeds fans. By the time he finally got the messages it was early evening and he returned to Carrington to find the drug testers were long gone. At around 4pm that same afternoon, Rio was spotted out shopping at department store Harvey Nichols, in Manchester's city centre. He, meanwhile, still insisted he was preoccupied with moving house.

Back on the field, Rio continued playing for Manchester United while awaiting a hearing on his case and, despite having plenty on his mind, produced some fine performances, much to the relief of Ferguson. The player admitted in the *Sun*: 'I know how important it is that I concentrate on my football despite everything that's been going on. This is a different time to what I've been used to in my career but you just have to deal with it. If I had let things get to me and hadn't been doing the business on the pitch I'm sure the manager would have dropped me. I wouldn't have expected anything else. When you are at a club like United, there is no room for passengers.'

Rio's two-day disciplinary hearing over the missed drugs test was eventually held in late December 2003. A three-man FA commission of chairman Barry Bright and his colleagues Frank Pattison and Peter Herd aimed to find out why one of England's most respected and talented footballers drove away from the Carrington training ground that day without being turned back to attend the drugs test. Rio attended each day of the proceedings held at Bolton's Reebok Stadium dressed in a dark, sombre suit and tie and accompanied by his counsel Robert Thwaites, QC. The commission heard evidence from the UK Sport testing team as they sought to piece together the chain of events that led to Rio contravening the drugs regulations.

On day two of the tribunal, Ferguson gave the impression that Rio would be found innocent and breezed in and out of the Reebok Stadium, saying nothing to waiting press but looking extremely pleased with himself. Later that day he made a point of telling journalists that Rio was definitely in the United team to play Tottenham at White Hart Lane the following day. Through his lawyer, Rio continued to insist that although he did forget to take the original test, he had in fact returned within two hours – but by then the testing team had departed. In a corridor near the hearings, Rio's agent Pini Zahavi was chewing on one of his favourite cigars. He insisted Rio was very relaxed about the proceedings. 'We have said from the start that Rio didn't do anything wrong and that is still what we believe,' explained Zahavi. 'Rio is okay. Obviously he would rather be somewhere else other than here, but he is handling things well. He is just looking forward to getting this over with and returning to his football.'

But the FA were convinced Rio had contravened the rules and he was found guilty of misconduct. He was handed an eight-month suspension and fined £50,000 for missing the drugs test. The suspension was due to start on 12 January and effectively ruled Rio out of the second half of United's Premiership campaign, as well as missing Euro 2004 in Portugal with England. The player was also ordered to pay all the FA's legal costs, estimated to be in the region of £100,000. Taking his own costs into account, Rio was facing a bill of at least £250,000. Rio wrote about his feelings on the situation in his column in the *Sun*: 'I was shocked and devastated when I heard the verdict. It hit me like a thunderbolt.'

The sentence produced a gasp from the assembled media at the Reebok Stadium, especially as many were predicting a ban of no more than three months. Rio was given 48 hours to ask for a written judgement and then another 14 days to appeal. In fact, United lodged an immediate appeal following the FA's decision, issuing only a brief statement – through an obviously angered club director and solicitor Maurice Watkins – when the verdict was announced. Ferguson remained impressively loyal to Rio and even talked about taking legal action against the FA. He told reporters: 'We'll need to assess the situation. It may not end with the FA – we may have to go to court and he's got a right to go to court to protect his reputation. The club would certainly support him.' But any plans Rio might have had to sue the FA were effectively blocked when outspoken FIFA president Sepp Blatter insisted that under the laws of the game Rio could not take his case to a civil court.

Others were not as sympathetic towards Rio as his manager. On hearing of the sentence, Dick Pound of the World Anti-Doping Agency said: 'I don't know what the disciplinary board heard that caused them to give a penalty that is only a third of the maximum. But it is clear they have rejected any suggestion that Ferdinand accidentally failed to take the test.'

Ironically, just before Rio's suspension took effect on 20 January 2004, he played one of his finest games for United in their 2–1 win at Tottenham, which took them to the top of the Premiership. Team-mate Mikael Silvestre was full of praise for Rio after the game: 'We knew Rio had a hard day and hard night after the hearing and he probably didn't get much sleep either but he was fantastic at Tottenham. That shows his character to come through and carry on playing. It's been a release for him. Playing is the best way to get away from his problems.'

The big question on everyone's lips in football was what on earth would Rio do with all his spare time now he'd been suspended from the game for eight months? He was preparing to appeal against the length of his playing ban as well as fronting an anti-drugs campaign in Manchester and his native south London. Then the tabloids spotted him out in a brand new £110,000 silver Bentley Continental GT sports coupe he'd just added to his collection – which already included a £36,000 BMW, a £168,000 Aston Martin, a £52,000 Lincoln Navigator and numerous other vehicles. Rio's latest toy had a 6-litre turbocharged 12-cylinder engine to help propel it from 0 to 60mph in just 4.7 seconds. There was even a built-in massager in the seats to help ease Rio's stress-ridden life.

On 18 March 2004, Rio withdrew his appeal against his suspension. The reasons for his about-turn were never fully explained, but it looked as if he was now going to have to swallow his punishment and hope he could revive his career when he was allowed to play again the following September.

United's European campaign came to a halt when they lost at home to Jose Mourinho's FC Porto in the second round of the Champions League. Many of the English club's fans believed that Rio's absence had considerably weakened the side. In the Premiership, results were not going United's way either and yet more fingers were being pointed at the defender's absence. But Rio did miss out on an FA Cup winner's medal when his United team-mates lifted the trophy after beating Millwall in the final at Cardiff's Millennium Stadium. It was the 11th time United had won the competition. A dazzling display by Ronaldo and a brace from Ruud van Nistelrooy helped them take the famous trophy back to Old Trafford.

16

Rio insisted he was doing constructive things during his suspension, including working for the charity Sport Relief. He visited a special football programme for children from a range of ethnic backgrounds in Ashton-under-Lyne, near Manchester, and enjoyed a kick around with some of those involved. He said: 'I'd like to think I've been using my spare time wisely. I've been training all the time with the rest of the lads but with not being involved in games I have also focused on other things.'

But an increasing number of Manchester United fans were wondering whether Rio's 'forgetfulness' in failing to do that drugs test had cost their team any chance of the two titles that really mattered – the Premiership and the Champions League. Although it must be said that Chelsea, who finished second behind Arsenal, had been bolstered by a £100 million outlay on top-class players funded by new billionaire owner Roman Abramovich. United's attack seemed as strong as ever with free-scoring van Nistelrooy but the midfield had been weakened by David Beckham's departure to Real Madrid and the defence had sorely missed Rio.

On the eve of the European Championships in Portugal in the summer of 2004 it was publicly revealed for the first time that Rio – still serving his eight-month ban – had made 'up to 20' phone calls to FA chief Mark Palios before his hearing, saying he was prepared to face a long club ban if he could play for England in Portugal. The rest of Europe was amazed at the harshness of the defender's sentence. Most other football associations usually only banned players in such circumstances for four or five months. Pini Zahavi commented: 'Rio should be playing in the European Championships and his ban would not happen in any other country than England.'

Just before the European Championships kicked off, Rio made a special journey to visit the England squad at their Manchester hotel to wish them luck. His old friend Frank Lampard recalled: 'Rio came to have dinner with us. Everyone knows how good a player Rio is and we will miss him. It must be hard for him at the moment. I know from talking to him that the closer we get to the matches the more frustrated he is feeling.'

June 2004 should have been one of the high spots of Rio's career; instead, he found himself out of the football limelight but still in the spotlight on the front pages of newspapers, where a series of kiss and tell stories threatened his relationship with Rebecca. Rio's penchant for slipping in and out of trouble seemed to know no boundaries. He badly needed to redeem his reputation and the only place he could do that was on the football pitch.

At the start of the new season, it was Manchester United's new signings Wayne Rooney and Cristiano Ronaldo who were grabbing all the headlines while Rio remained suspended until September. And defensive recruit Argentinian Gabriel Heinze quickly won over the Old Trafford faithful with a number of superb performances for the club.

Finally, on 20 September 2004, Rio made his first appearance since his suspension ended, in United's clash with old rivals Liverpool. It was now 363 days since that fateful day when he'd missed the drugs test sparking his suspension. Rio was welcomed back like the prodigal son by the diehards of the Stretford End, who have always known when to throw a protective arm around their own, particularly those – Eric Cantona, David Beckham and Roy Keane – whom they perceive to be have been victimised because they play for United.

United boss Alex Ferguson made a point of telling a packed press conference before the Liverpool clash: 'I've never had more admiration for a lad than I have for Rio for the way he handled his suspension. He has been absolutely terrific. Many at the club shared Ferguson's opinion. Gary Neville said: 'He certainly surprised me because I never believed anybody could show that degree of professionalism during those eight months. The way he came to training every day, the way he kept his focus. I half expected him to disappear on holiday until the following pre-season.'

Neville even pushed for Rio to get a rapid-fire return to the England team for their World Cup qualifying campaign match against Wales in early October. 'I know what Rio brings to Manchester United and England. In 2002 he and Sol Campbell were the best central defensive pairing in the World Cup, and Rio has a case for being considered one of the best in the world.' On the other hand, some observers from outside Old Trafford believed that Rio's training, charity duties and habit of popping up at regular intervals to remind everyone of his sense of injustice in the *Sun* showed a cynical disregard for the rules of the game.

Rio himself seemed to know that he owed both Ferguson and England boss Eriksson 'big time' – or at least that's what he told journalists. Within weeks of the player's return to Manchester United's team, Eriksson hailed Rio as the best centre-half he had ever seen so few people were surprised when the defender found himself back in the England team to face Wales. Rio said: 'For your managers to be showing that sort of confidence in putting you straight back into two great teams breeds confidence in yourself. Mr Eriksson has been great. He put his name to a statement supporting me and spoke to me a few times on the phone and having those sort of touches was a great help to me during the ban.'

But Rio couldn't avoid controversy for long. He was back on the front pages, 'exposed' for being out clubbing hours after being given leave to miss United's Champions League away match against Sparta Prague for his grandmother's funeral. Some were wondering if – not when – Rio would ever learn to keep his head down. It's not known how Ferguson reacted to Rio's antics. It was rumoured that some of United's most senior players were unhappy with Rio's behaviour, but for the moment his place in the team remained unquestioned. One observer seemed to sum up the player's character when he explained: 'Rio is Rio. He seems to be a law unto himself. Only time will tell if his career can keep surviving the onslaught of stories about his off-the-field behaviour.'

Meanwhile, already 11 points behind Arsenal in the race for the title, United needed to keep winning to prevent their bitter rivals from North London reaching a milestone of 50 Premiership games unbeaten and claw back lost ground at the top of the table. On the European front, United only got as far as the second round where they were knocked out by AC Milan after suffering 1–0 defeats at home and away. The Manchester United winning machine seemed to be faltering somewhat. And it looked as though their record signing might be rocking the boat.

In April 2005 he was spotted in two London restaurants with Chelsea chief executive Peter Kenyon. In one photograph, former United executive Kenyon appeared to be dining with Rio and Pini Zahavi. Ferguson was reported in one newspaper to be 'incandescent' with rage after seeing the pictures. The United manager had already accused Kenyon of treating his former club United with contempt.

Many were asking how a man as experienced and shrewd as Zahavi could invite his most valuable client to a London restaurant in which Kenyon was eating on a Saturday night without realising the publicity it would create. For the moment, that question would have to remain unanswered or simply a matter of coincidence. As usual Rio brushed off the rumours that he might be off to Chelsea.

United ended the 2004-05 season a disappointing third in the Premiership behind Arsenal and newly crowned champions Chelsea. Many were starting to wonder if the club's incredible run of success was grinding to a halt. Then it emerged that Ferdinand and Zahavi were involved in some protracted talks with United over Rio's contract. He was demanding £120,000 a week. Significantly, Ferguson fed the press a ringing endorsement of Rio, saying: 'I do not blame him. He wants to stay with us.'

Ferguson also refused to criticise Zahavi, who later said: 'Of course he didn't say anything. Alex and I are friends and he trusts me.' But the controversy surrounding Rio's 'encounters' with Kenyon had already highlighted the close relationship which now existed between Zahavi and United rivals Chelsea. The Israeli super agent's world had turned around since he first delivered Roman Abramovich to Chelsea in the summer of 2003. Having subsequently played a part in bringing in Kenyon and coach Jose Mourinho to Stamford Bridge, Zahavi was now more than just an advisor to the West London club, who'd just won their first championship in 50 years.

However, the ever-canny Zahavi continued to insist: 'Rio loves it at Manchester United and wants to stay there, but it depends on United, not on him, whether that happens. Everybody has to give a little. It's called negotiation. Rio deserves to earn, if not more than the other top central defenders in the world, then at least the same.'

But by late June 2005 Rio and Zahavi had still failed to agree a new contract with United. The club's fans were astounded that he would dare hold out for £130,000 a week considering the loyalty shown to him during his drug test problems. On 4 July, he was even booed by supporters during a 5–1 friendly win at Clyde. Many called him 'greedy'.

A few days later the *Mail on Sunday* reported that Alex Ferguson was furious with Rio for refusing to sign an improved contract offer of £110,000 a week and was intending to demand that the England defender make a public pledge of loyalty to the club. Rio was now holding out for £120,000 a week but United were refusing to go that high. Ferguson told the paper: 'He says he wants to stay so he should say that now, That would take away any lingering suspicions and doubts.'

In the middle of all the Manchester United controversy was the Glazer family of American multi-millionaires, who'd just completed a highly contentious takeover at Old Trafford. During United's Asia tour – which was marred by low attendances and questions about the absence of skipper Roy Keane – there were face-to-face clashes between supporters and members of the Glazer family. Fans stormed a VIP area in Beijing to vent their anger at Bryan Glazer, who was travelling with the official club party. Two men broke through a security cordon but had a reasonably civil conversation with Glazer, whose family were part of a takeover that had left United with debts of almost £100 million.

At the beginning of August, Manchester United suddenly announced they had won the wages stand-off with Rio when he agreed to sign a new four-year deal worth around £5 million a year, which effectively ended months of uncertainty over his future. It is believed that Rio settled for a weekly wage just in excess of £100,000. Rio privately told friends and associates he hoped that the settlement would mark the end of his summer of abuse from fans.

17

Rio and his England team-mates received a major setback when they were thrashed 4–1 in a friendly by Denmark during the summer of 2005 and then beaten 1–0 by Northern Ireland in a World Cup qualifying game in September. The tabloids turned up the pressure on coach Sven-Goran Eriksson to drop Rio because England's place in the 2006 World Cup Finals in Germany appeared to be under threat and his performances in both games were poor.

After the Denmark defeat, Eriksson insisted the England squad sat through a painful re-run of the game with their mistakes highlighted to learn from. 'We all agreed it was unacceptable,' explained Rio. 'I set my standards very high and that was nowhere near the standard. It was a case of it finally hitting home and showing us first-hand exactly what he wasn't happy with. We were disappointed and embarrassed as players.'

But it was the 1–0 defeat by Northern Ireland that turned up the pressure even more on Eriksson to drop Rio for the next World Cup qualifying game against Austria at Old Trafford at the beginning of October. 'Humiliation' was the most popular word used on the sports pages and it summed up the public's reaction to the shock defeat. Henry Winter in the *Daily Telegraph* wrote: 'England slumped to their most embarrassing defeat since the 1981 reverse to Norway. Bereft of thought and fight, strangled by a system they clearly did not enjoy, England's players lost their first qualifier under Sven-Goran Eriksson, who faces an autumn of deepening discontent. "Sack the Swede" chanted England's fans.'

A few weeks later, Rio rushed to the defence of under-fire teenager Wayne Rooney whose red card in United's opening UEFA Champions League Group D game at Villarreal CF sparked even more criticism of the 19-year-old's temperament. 'Wayne has worked very hard on his discipline and improved it no end since coming to United,' explained a very fatherly Rio. 'He plays on the edge and that is important to his impact on a game, but Wayne is already being booked less regularly for United than he was at Everton.'

On the domestic front, Manchester United's opening to the 2005-06 campaign seemed to be heading in a healthy direction with three straight wins but two draws and a defeat at home to Blackburn Rovers on 24 September were a mighty blow to United's attempt to keep up with all-conquering Chelsea, who started the season with nine wins on the trot and were already seven points clear of the rest of the pack by mid-October. And Rio couldn't put a foot right, or so it seemed. When United travelled to Fulham and won 3–2, he was heavily criticised for being at fault for both of Fulham's goals. The season never seemed to get going. After a comfortable 6–0 win over Debreceni VSC in the qualifying round of the Champions League, United crashed out at the first group stage with only one win to their name. They were knocked out of the FA Cup by arch-rivals Liverpool and finished only third in the league. Rio also suffered the blow of being sent off for the first time in his career. Playing in midfield against Blackburn, he picked up two yellow cards in a minute, the second for an uncharacteristic lunge on Robbie Savage that saw the Welshman carried off on a stretcher. But there was some consolation for Rio: after waiting 140 matches, he finally opened his goal-scoring account at United against Wigan on 14 December and then followed that up with goals against West Brom on Boxing Day and Liverpool towards the end of January. There was more joy against Wigan when United beat them 4–0 in the Carling Cup final at the Millennium Stadium. It was a comfortable afternoon for Rio and another medal but he hadn't come to Old Trafford to win the League Cup.

With speculation rife that he might be dropped from the England team, Rio once again admitted his form had fallen below his own high standards. He said: 'You have to show the strength of character to come through the difficult times. I know I have got that and I know my team-mates have it as well.' Rio insisted that the embarrassing defeat in Northern Ireland would motivate the England team. He explained: 'Nobody wants to be associated with failing to qualify for the World Cup finals. I cannot imagine the shame of it. There is a huge responsibility on all of us to get England through. It would be one of the biggest disasters in sports history if we blew it and we must make sure it does not happen.'

By the time of England's crucial World Cup qualifier against Austria on 8 October, Eriksson bowed to pressure from all directions and dropped Rio from the heart of his defence. There was a growing feeling that he had been under-performing for both club and country on at least the previous half a dozen games. Chelsea skipper John Terry and Arsenal veteran Sol Campbell were paired for the Old Trafford clash with Austria but, as has so often been the case, Rio had a lucky break when Campbell was injured early in the second half and he came on as substitute. England scraped through 1–0 and that evening Holland defeated the Czechs, effectively handing England automatic qualification for the World Cup with the best runners-up record.

Four days later, England faced group leaders Poland at Old Trafford with Rio restored to the side. This time England took control from the start and the United defender never put a foot wrong as his side upped the tempo of the game and ended up comfortable 2–1 winners with a greatly improved performance to go top of their group above the Poles. And in November 2005 England secured a gripping 3–2 triumph over long-standing rivals Argentina, with Rio having to be on his mettle from the outset against the spirited South Americans. Now the World Cup in Germany was beckoning and Rio was going to have to fight for his place in the England side. Many saw it as healthy competition and he had a habit of reacting well to this sort of pressure so, unless he had injury problems, Rio was on the verge of re-establishing himself on the world stage.

As so often happens with England, controversy surrounded the World Cup campaign from the moment

Eriksson named his squad. With Michael Owen struggling for form and Wayne Rooney carrying an injury, the Swede was expected to name an experienced fourth striker alongside Peter Crouch. Instead he gambled on Arsenal reserve Theo Walcott who had yet to make his Premiership debut. Immediately, doubts were raised about England's chances and they didn't improve when the tournament got under way.

England started their Group B campaign with a stuttering 1–0 win over Paraguay in Frankfurt. It looked as though it would be comfortable when Carlos Gamarra deflected David Beckham's free-kick past his own keeper in the third minute but in the second half it needed plenty of concentration by Rio and John Terry – the partnership Eriksson preferred throughout the tournament – to hang on to the points.

Their second performance wasn't much more convincing even though they made it through to the last 16. England created plenty of chances against Trinidad and Tobago but it took goals in the last seven minutes from Peter Crouch and Steven Gerrard to secure the victory. The good news for Eriksson was that Rooney was able to come off the bench for his first appearance and another of his 'gambles', Aaron Lennon, looked impressive when he too came on at the hour mark. It was England's eighth straight win since the defeat by Northern Ireland, only two short of their record set nearly 100 years before.

With their progress secured, England's hopes of a trouble-free third match against Sweden ended after just a minute when Owen's right knee buckled under him as he tried to pass and he was stretchered off. The team kept their composure and went ahead after 35 minutes when Rio's former West Ham team-mate Joe Cole chested down a clearance and smashed a dipping volley past the keeper from 35 yards.

With Cole and Rooney in irresistible form, England looked set to kick on but just after half time Marcus Allback found space at a corner and headed Sweden's equaliser. Five minutes later, after picking up a knock, Rio was replaced by Campbell and watched from the sidelines when Cole was involved again, providing the cross for Gerrard to head England in front with five minutes to go. But they couldn't hang on to the lead and Henrik Larsson earned the Swedes a point in added time.

With England's defence not at its best, Eriksson played Michael Carrick in a holding role just in front of Rio and Terry against Ecuador. Even then an early mistake by the Chelsea defender almost allowed the South Americans to go ahead but Carlos Tenorio's shot deflected off Ashley Cole and flew on to the bar. Rooney was becoming increasingly frustrated after being asked to plough a lone furrow up front and it took a trade-mark free-kick from David Beckham to win the match, making the midfielder the first England player to score in three World Cup finals.

England had not played well in the tournament and knew they would have to raise their game in the quarter-final if they were to get past Portugal. But hopes faded when Beckham limped out of the action just after half time and Rooney's suspect temperament got the better of him once more and he was sent off in the 62nd minute for stamping on Ricardo Carvalho. With temperatures soaring close to 30C, England had to batten down the hatches and with the fans roaring them on, they produced their most passionate display of the tournament. Rio and Terry shut up shop at the back despite being under constant pressure and they saw out the match and half an hour's extra time without conceding. But as so often in the past, faced with a penalty shoot-out, England were found wanting. Hargreaves was the only England player to score and misses by Lampard, Gerrard and Carragher saw them crash out of the World Cup. The defeat ended Eriksson's reign as manager and he was replaced by Steve McClaren.

David Beckham also stood down as captain and speculation immediately arose that Rio would be given the armband, but many people had doubts. When the BBC website assessed the various candidates they pointed to his lapses in concentration and said: 'It will be better to leave Ferdinand to keep his mind on defensive duties rather than clutter it up with greater responsibility.'

The World Cup campaign had been another let down for the whole country and a couple of years later Rio admitted: 'I think we got caught up in the whole thing. There was a big show around the whole England squad. It was like a theatre unfolding and football became a secondary element. People were worrying more about what people were wearing than the games. We were in the bubble ourselves. In Baden Baden, walking around, there were paparazzi everywhere, our families were there. Looking back, it was like a circus. As a squad, we were a bit too open, going out in and around Baden Baden, probably had too much contact with families. That's just my opinion. You're in a tournament and you don't get many tournaments in your career. You have to be focused.'

18

After the disappointment of the World Cup and what had been a frustrating few years by their standards for Manchester United, together with far too many visits to the front pages of tabloid newspapers, Rio's career finally started to live up to all its early promise as he and his club responded brilliantly to the threat posed by Arsenal, Liverpool and especially the billionaire-backed Chelsea.

With Wayne Rooney, Louis Saha and Cristiano Ronaldo scoring goals for fun, Rio picked up his second Premiership medal in 2006-2007. United crashed home 83 goals in the league campaign, 19 more than second-placed Chelsea, while Rio and his impressive new central defensive partner Nemanja Vidic provided something of a fortress at the back. To the joy of United fans, the title was clinched by a victory over Manchester City. 'The younger players are starting to mature and get better,' Alex Ferguson explained. 'We were a team that was growing but we are a few years older now and there is a maturity in our performances this season.' He could well have cited Rio as a prime example.

In the Champions League, United enjoyed what Ferguson described as 'the greatest night in Europe at Old Trafford' when they thrashed Roma 7–1. But maybe they peaked too soon because, in the semi-final, after beating AC Milan 3–2 at home, they went down 3–0 in the San Siro. Rio was injured for that match and could only watch from the bench as Vidic, himself only just back from a broken collarbone, and a makeshift defence struggled in the pouring rain. There was another disappointment in the FA Cup final where Chelsea gained revenge for being pipped to the Premiershp with a win after extra time at the newly restored Wembley Stadium. Rio and Vidic had snuffed out the threat of Didier Drogba all afternoon and Vidic almost grabbed the winner in the last minute of normal time, but his header went just over the bar. But in the dying minutes of extra time, Drogba finally managed to shake off the shackles and sent Chelsea fans home happy.

Rio had been impressive throughout the campaign and was deservedly named in the PFA team of the season. He and Vidic were proving to be the best United pairing since the days of Steve Bruce and Gary Pallister and after a shaky start to the new season that saw the Reds pick up only two points from the first three matches, they kept six successive clean sheets to get their title defence back on track plus a couple in the Champions League. Rio opened his Champions League goal account for United when he headed in Ryan Giggs's free-kick to put them into the lead against Dynamo Kiev and on the way to a 4–2 victory.

Ferguson's predictions of his side's growing maturity were borne out as they overhauled the pack to take the

Premiership title for the second year in a row with the lowest number of goals conceded in the division while again scoring 80 at the other end. But the Old Trafford boss badly wanted the Champions League trophy that had eluded him since 1999. After negotiating the group stages, United couldn't have faced a more challenging run in. The quarter-finals set them against Roma, which they came through without conceding a goal. In the semi-final, they faced the mighty Barcelona and held them to a goalless draw at the Nou Camp with Ronaldo missing a penalty. With Gary Neville a long term injury and Ryan Giggs not selected, Rio was captain for the second leg and described by the *Guardian* as 'unyielding' in a titanic clash that was decided by Paul Scholes' 14th minute strike from 25 yards. United were in the final, where Chelsea awaited. It would be Rio against his former West Ham pal Frank Lampard at the Luzhniki stadium in Moscow.

Once more Rio had the armband for the greatest game of his career so far. He admitted: 'I tried to sleep in the afternoon as I normally do before games but I think I got about 20 minutes. It tells you how much bigger this game was. There was huge pressure and I knew that the team that dealt with it best would come out the winners. To me it was the stuff of dreams. Who would have thought when I was cleaning Tony Cottee's and Harry Redknapp's boots that one day I would lead a team out in the Champions League final?'

The script almost seemed to be written ahead of time. It was 50 years since many of United's great 'Busby Babes' side had perished in the Munich air crash and 40 years since the Reds became the first English side to win Europe's major club competition. But on a rain-sodden night, Chelsea weren't ready to bow to history and contributed to a memorable final. Ronaldo headed United in front after 26 minutes but just before half time Michael Essien's shot deflected off Vidic and Ferdinand into the path of Lampard who grabbed the equaliser. 'Lamps' goal was a sucker punch,' Rio said, 'but we weathered the storm in the second half.' As the drama continued, Drogba was sent off for a slap on Vidic and even after 120 minutes the sides couldn't be separated. It would be a penalty shoot-out.

At 2–2 Ronaldo saw his spot kick saved by Petr Cech. Rio admitted: 'So many different things go through your mind when Cristiano missed his penalty. You start to think: he has done so well all season and is it going to end like this? You are begging for one of their players to miss.' And one did; John Terry stepped up with the chance to win the Champions League but slipped on the wet surface and his shot hit the outside of the post. As the shoot-out went into sudden death, Salomon Kalou and Ryan Giggs netted, but Nicolas Anelka's effort was saved by Edwin van der Sar and United were champions.

Sir Bobby Charlton, a survivor of the Munich crash, led United up to collect the trophy and Rio called Giggs up alongside him to lift the huge cup aloft. It was the kind of moment the kid from Peckham had often visualised but never dared to hope would come true. He said: 'Playing for Man United is a great achievement in itself but to be one of the players lucky enough to lift the Champions League trophy puts it into another stratosphere. Sir Bobby was very emotional in the dressing room afterwards and the most poignant thing for me was him coming up to me and

saying "Well done, you deserved it." Fate seemed to play a big part. Giggsy broke Bobby's appearance record in the European Cup final and it was 50 years since Munich – so maybe it was written in the stars.'

19

Rio's trophy cabinet was filling up but he still wasn't immune from criticism. After United were beaten 2–1 in the UEFA Supercup by Zenit St Petersburg, Martin Samuel wrote in *The Times*: 'Certainly, United appeared to be taken aback by the potential of their opponents and allowed Zenit's intelligent forwards far too much space. Rio Ferdinand was particularly guilty. Fabio Capello, the watching England manager, must have left contented that he made the right choice about his England captain, if not entirely happy with the wider implication of what he saw. John Terry has his faults, but falling asleep at the wheel is not one of them.'

But Rio was to have the last word as the season progressed with United picking up their third consecutive Premiership title, losing only four matches on the way to collecting 90 points. He also popped another winners' medal alongside his impressive collection when United beat Ecuadorian side Liga de Quito to take the Club World Cup in Japan despite having Vidic sent off, and added further to his haul when the Reds lifted the League Cup, beating

Spurs 4–1 in yet another penalty shoot-out after the final finished goalless.

Once again the Champions League provided Rio with some of his most vivid memories. United went through the group stages unbeaten and then overcame Inter Milan without conceding a goal. Things looked tricky when Porto came to Old Trafford and earned a 2–2 draw in the first leg of the quarter final. Rio missed that match through injury but returned for the second meeting after which most of the attention was on Ronaldo's sensational 40-yard strike that won the game for United. But Rio and his fellow defenders held firm and Matt Lawton reported in the *Daily Mail*: 'In Ferdinand and Vidic, Ferguson still has a defensive partnership as reliable as any on the planet.' Not that the Old Trafford boss needed telling. He said before the match: 'Rio always makes a difference when he's in the team. It's the experience and the quality he has in his game. It will also see us back to the partnership of Ferdinand and Vidic, which has been the cornerstone of great defensive performances this season.'

The win set up a classic semi-final against London rivals Arsenal. John O'Shea scored the only goal of the game at Old Trafford when Rio had to come off towards the end having taken a crack in the ribs, but he recovered in time for the second leg when United dominated proceedings at the Emirates and clinched a 3–1 win. Two of the biggest clubs in the world, Manchester United and Barcelona, would now go head to head in the final played in the magnificent Stadio Olimpico in Rome.

United had set their hearts on becoming the first side to defend the trophy but after a bright start they were

outshone by the Catalan superstars. Messi, Xavi and Iniesta were almost unplayable and the trio inspired the Spanish giants to a 2–0 win. Rio tried to hide his disappointment but admitted United had not played well, adding: 'You've got to give credit to Barcelona, they played well. We needed to play our best football and we didn't produce it. The first goal was a sucker punch, we'd had some good chances. They were two soft goals and we could have done better leading up to them and I could have done better with my positioning but we've got no excuses, they were a better team.'

The defeat in Rome marked something of an end of an era at United who allowed Cristiano Ronaldo to move to Real Madrid for an astonishing, world record £80 million fee. But while they were not the same potent force at the start of World Cup season, they nevertheless were still one of the favourites to take the Premiership title. Rio picked up a back injury that restricted his appearances and on his comeback against Hull City, he was sent off and suspended for four matches. A return of the back injury meant he also missed United's League Cup final victory over Aston Villa.

But Alex Ferguson assured anxious England fans that Rio's injury wasn't long term and shouldn't hamper his chances of leading his country to the World Cup finals in South Africa. After the disappointment of failing to qualify for Euro 2008, England had turned to Fabio Capello to take over as manager and the Italian transformed the national side. They lost only one of their ten qualifying games, going down 1–0 in Ukraine long after they had already booked their place in the finals. Along the way they had scored 34 goals while only conceding six.

Rio was impressed by Capello, comparing him favourably with his Manchester United boss, probably the highest accolade a manager can receive. 'He stacks up against all the managers at club level in the world,' Rio said. 'I don't know the real Alex Ferguson. When he comes to football, he's probably a totally different animal to when he's at home with his wife and grandchildren. They're not here to be buddies, talk about pastimes or be great friends. They're here to win football matches. That's where this manager [Capello] comes from. When we win games, the manager here is still likely to point out the things we're not doing well.

'He's very, very clear. He has a certain way that he wants us to play. He'll let us know if we're not carrying out those methods. I just think that it was very much, "I'm the boss and this is what is happening". This regime is very water-tight. We've seen from other England managers, Kevin Keegan even before Steve McClaren, saying we should wear our hearts on our sleeves but nowadays you have to be a structured team and nullify the threats of other teams. You need to be calm and compact. We've got a very business-like state of mind and that's come from the manager and the staff he's got around. It's a new way of thinking. There's a winning mentality.'

After many times in the early part of his career when off-the-field controversy seemed set to damage Rio's progress, it was the front-page antics of John Terry that led to the Manchester United defender being made the captain of England for the 2010 World Cup. Rio had led the side on a number of occasions but Capello had settled on Terry as his full time skipper until the Chelsea man's name was splashed all over the newspapers for having an affair with the ex-girlfriend of former Chelsea and England team-mate Wayne Bridge. That was too much of a threat to the dressing room harmony the Italian values so highly, so he stripped Terry of the armband and handed it to Rio.

At last the tall, skinny kid from the Friary Estate was fulfilling the prediction of those West Ham pundits who claimed he would one day follow in the footsteps of Bobby Moore. Harry Redknapp, the man who had guided Rio's early career, said in the *Sun*: 'I have watched Rio and a number of the other young lads we had at West Ham grow up as players and men to carve great careers in the game. Even from the age of 15 I had no doubt that he would mature to become the best defender in Europe. He has been there and done it at club level – Champions League glory. Premier League titles. Now the World Cup is the final piece of the jigsaw for him.'

Redknapp revealed that on hearing of Rio's appointment, he sent the player a text saying 'Do it with class – the way Bobby Moore did. And bring the World Cup back to England.' Rio's mentor is confident his protégé has what it takes to do just that, saying: 'Rio will be a fine captain of captains and if we do go all the way in South Africa don't be surprised if he wipes his dirty hands before picking up the cup – just like Bobby did in 1966.'